You Cannot Turn Away

POEMS IN TAMIL BY

Cheran

EDITED AND TRANSLATED INTO ENGLISH BY

Chelva Kanaganayakam

I0894067

Tamil text © 2011 R Cheran
Translation and Introduction © 2011 Chelva Kanaganayakam

Except for purposes of review, no part of this
book may be reproduced in any form without
prior permission of the publisher.

We acknowledge the support of the Canada Council for the Arts for our publishing program and the Government of Ontario through the Ontario Arts Council.

Canada Council for the Arts | Conseil des Arts du Canada

ONTARIO ARTS COUNCIL
CONSEIL DES ARTS DE L'ONTARIO

Cover image: *Sisters* by Chikmath F V,
Courtesy Ayya Art Galleries, Chennai
www.ayyaart.com

Cover design by Cynthia Griffioen
Page design by Eugine Vincent (Karuna), Digi Media Creations, Toronto

Library and Archives Canada Cataloguing in Publication

Cheran, R.
You cannot turn away / by R. Cheran ; translated by Chelva Kanaganayakam.

Poems.
Text in English and Tamil.
ISBN 978-1-894770-74-3

I. Kanaganayakam, Chelva, 1952- II. Title.

PS8605.H463Y68 2011 C894.8'11172 C2011-903253-8

Printed in Canada by Coach House Printing

TSAR Publications
P. O. Box 6996, Station A
Toronto, Ontario M5W 1X7
Canada

www.tsarbooks.com

Contents

INTRODUCTION

CHELVA KANAGANAYAKAM

A recent poem by Cheran, written sometime after the carnage of May 2009, which marked a radical shift in the ethnic politics of Sri Lanka, expresses a deeply subjective and nuanced response to the contemporary scene, using a diction that is shorn of all embellishment, and is both allusive and suggestive despite its self-consciously epigrammatic style:

Parched ocean
Silent land
Nameless kin

This untitled poem remains a challenge to the translator, largely because for the Tamil reader, the original suggests a great deal about the specific cluster of events in Mullivaikkal in the Northeastern region of Mullaitivu that culminated in the defeat of the LTTE in May 2009. Although the poem, even in Tamil, remains abstract and generalized, for the reader who knows the cultural and political scene and is competent in the original language, the specificity and intentionality are abundantly clear. The poem expresses a deep concern about cultural loss, occasioned by violence, dispersal and death. A more literal (although very effective) translation of the poem, which appeared in a recent collection of poems, reads in the following manner:

the sea is without water
tamil is without land
kinship is without a name[i]

Here the translation is more expressive of a particular moment of violence, upheaval and fragmentation. A sea without the translucence of water is reminiscent of Macbeth's famous line: "multitudinous seas incarnadine, making the green one red." The sea (a recurring trope in Cheran's work) is a site of struggle but also one that suggests comfort, life and livelihood. In the second line, the translation draws attention to a specific kind of cultural identity where the land and landscape are associated with both language and ethnicity. Mullaitivu is one of the many places where Tamils lived for centuries, and yet the poem asserts that this moment of violence has deeply affected the linguistic and cultural identity of a people as a whole. Given the widespread presence of Tamil-speaking people in various lands, the line is deliberately enigmatic. In the final line, there is an ominous projection of the future, a time when kith and kin, dispersed in alien lands, will fail to recognize each other, resulting in a community of "familiar strangers". My own version is, admittedly, more generalized and abstract, largely because Cheran's poetry, for the most part, oscillates between the specific and the general. The fact that the poem lends itself so well to both versions is in itself a measure of the richness of the original and the strength of Cheran's poems in general.

For those who are familiar with Cheran's poetry, this poem (and for that matter, almost all of his more recent poems included in the final section of this collection) would appear to be both familiar and surprisingly different. They are familiar in that they continue certain thematic preoccupations that have been quite central to his work from the beginning. Issues of cultural identity, political stability, nation and nationalism, diasporic life, fragility of human relations, and many others run through his entire work. The recent poems are different in that they recognize the need to use a very different diction, speak with a different voice. Gone are the lilting rhythms of his early poetry and the modernist narratives of his later work. May 2009 marked a watershed in political life, and the poet's work seems to imply that the poetic imagination, responding to the present, cannot simply rehearse the forms of the past. Noticeably absent are certain kinds of metaphors that are present in his earlier poetry. Poetic forms that seemed necessary and relevant in the past are no longer effective, and the poet alters his style to give expression to a different sense of the world. Cheran's struggle to understand and relate to the political vicissitudes of his time must be seen together with his self-relexivity and his search for adequate poetic forms.

At the very outset it is important to recognize that Cheran is the product of a conflict-ridden Sri Lanka. This might be stating the obvious, since it is common knowledge that in Sri Lanka from the 1970s until the defeat of the LTTE in 2009, the dominant concern among the people, both Tamils and Sinhalese, was ethnic conflict. Towards the latter part of that decade, unrest among the Tamils, particularly the youth, became increasingly common, eventually leading to the rise of militant groups among the Tamils that sought violent means to counter what they saw as the hegemony of the state. While Cheran himself was not affiliated with any particular movement, and was often critical of the stances adopted by various political organizations, he lived and functioned in a culture that was deeply politicized. Politics was thus the overarching concern of many writers of this time, including Cheran. Unlike poets who started writing earlier and encountered the transformation of society in the 1970s and 1980s, Cheran came into his own as a poet during this time. Politics and violence in the country shaped his craft, his imagination, and his consciousness. Any serious evaluation of Cheran's poetry should take into consideration the effect of having to live and function in a world in which politics and the violence it gave rise to permeated each and every aspect of life. Cheran's poetry demonstrates the process of not only learning from the literary traditions of the past, but also reshaping them to address the urgency of the present. Both the politics and poetics of his work are determined by the turmoil and upheaval of conflict.

It is common knowledge that some measure of political uncertainty was often present in post-colonial Sri Lanka. Even a cursory look at the history of postcolonial Sri Lanka would confirm that manifestations of political dissatisfaction were common, both among the Sinhalese and the Tamils. The ethnic conflict of 1958 and the insurgency of 1971 were obvious cases in point. The Tamil poets who wrote in the 1960s and 1970s were not unmindful of the political backdrop and the effects of political decisions on social and cultural life. But political uncertainty was only one aspect of a new postcolonial nation. There were many other concerns for the Tamils that were seen as urgent, including caste, class, economic disparity, regionalism, and so forth. The poets of these early decades thus worked with a number of concerns and their poetry was inevitably eclectic and sometimes hermetic as well. Their poetry was socially conscious, and often quite progressive, but it implicitly endorsed the notion of aesthetic distance.

Cheran grew up in this context, and his early influences included the work of his father, Mahakavi, whose poetry was path-breaking in its ability to merge a distinctly modernist sensibility with traditional metrical forms of poetry. Cheran himself acknowledges in an interview the deep impact of his father's poetry, and his own habit of memorizing large chunks of his father's poetry and then reciting them in public places. He also claims that at a certain stage in his career, the influence became less prominent, as his own voice became clear to him.[ii] Among other things, his father's poetry taught him the rhythms of language, and the prosodic forms of traditional Tamil poetry. Orality was central to Mahakavi's work, and if Cheran's poetry continues to have a strong oral dimension, it is probably because he recognized the potential in Mahakavi's work to appeal to a large audience. In any account that relates to Cheran's intellectual genealogy, it is necessary to emphasize that it was his father who played a major role in steering a tradition of conventional poetry to one that was socially conscious and one that accommodated the idiom of ordinary speech. Mahakavi's poetry and his plays enabled a distinct break from the tradition of Tamil poetry from Tamil Nadu in that it was neither experimental nor entirely conventional, but one that was receptive to both in a distinctly Sri Lankan way. Mahakavi was writing at a time when poetry was still the possession of a small group of writers and critics, and his own accommodation of the local and the folk was shaped within the framework of conventional poetry. Even in a famous poem such as "Therum Thingalum" where the speech rhythms interact most forcefully with poetic diction, the effect of artifice leans towards convention. To say this does not take away from the major contribution of Mahakavi: it simply highlights the fact that he belonged to a particular time and a particular place.

Cheran also records in other places how his consciousness was shaped by Marxist thinkers, both local and international, whose perspectives were particularly meaningful in a class-conscious and caste-conscious Tamil society. Says Cheran:

> My association with an important representative of the Communist Party and a charismatic speaker Comrade V. Ponnambalam gave me a sense of the importance of contesting both class and caste structures. During this period, around 1973-74 two of my poems appeared in the newspaper run by the Communist Party.... In 1975-76 Mao's writing became available. Another close friend N. Murugadas was actively involved in the Communist Party led by Shanmugathasan. He was a passionate reader of literature as well. Through him I was introduced to both Mao's writings and the literary journal *Kasadathapara*.[iii]

Marxism, however, remained one aspect of his early vision. The lyricism, gentle irony, sense of community and belonging, and the love and eroticism of his early poetry are a testimony to the multiplicity of the early 1970s. This was, however, a time of learning for Cheran, a time of shaping his craft. The lyricism of some of his early poems is a clear indication of the influence of a poetic environment that may have been influenced by ideas of social reform but was equally conscious of the need for aesthetic distance in poetry.

If one were to think of *Maranothul Valvom*, an anthology put together by Cheran et al in 1984 as a turning point, the title itself (We live amidst death) alerts one to a complete transformation of sensibility. This was one year after Cheran had published his first volume of poems, titled *Irandavathu Suriya Uthayam* (The Second Sunrise) which points to the burning of the Jaffna Public Library.[iv] This title is significant in that it signals a particular urgency, a direct engagement with the political and cultural context of the time. The introduction to *Maranothul Valvom*, written by Cheran, is a valuable guide to his thought and his poetry. In this he records the impact of living in a context in which the extraordinary had become the ordinary. Among the observations that Cheran (one of the editors who writes the preface) makes, one needs to note in particular that the collection was seen as part of a larger cultural scene in which literature, together with other cultural forms, was being embraced by the public as a constitutive element in a larger framework that involved nationalism and ethnic identity. As he puts it, 'in our context, poetry is hardly for silent reading or for the sole enjoyment of intellectuals. It must appeal to the common person.'[v] Poetry, together with fiction and drama, now had a much more vital role to play, and this collection points to a radical shift in sensibility and in poetic practice. A new vision, a new style, and a new urgency had entered the literary scene.

The next collection, *Yaman*, published in 1984, sets the tone of despair and death that now becomes a crucial element in life. During the last three decades, Cheran's personal and public life have undergone many changes, and his current status as an academic and a diasporic poet in Canada are a far cry from his early life in Sri Lanka, but he has remained very much a "political" poet, a product of a time of political and cultural upheaval in Sri Lanka. Although Cheran has written about love and exile, for instance, and writers such as Sundara Ramaswamy have alluded to the strength of such poems, his ongoing concern has been with the impact of politics in the social and cultural life of the Tamil people.[vi]

Cheran's poetry as a whole, however, defies any easy compartmentalization. From the very beginning, the challenges were many. In the first instance, it was never very easy for the poet to define his own role within the conflict-ridden state. While the commitment to some form of Tamil identity appears to have been a common thread in all the poetry, the particular contours of this commitment were far from clear. In the murky waters of ethnic strife, a simple binary along ethnic lines was never easy. The poet demonstrates in several poems the need to see beyond ethnicity to human relations, to friendships, and to the suffering on both sides. Equally important, the resistance among militant groups was never seen as unified. In his own life, Cheran's refusal to stand behind any particular stance meant, quite often, living on the edge. There is a poem in his corpus that is significantly titled, "A Poem That Should Not Have Been Written." It is a poem that expresses the deep disillusionment of a militant group attacking Sinhalese civilians and the awareness that even the most lofty ideals might mask cruelty. In such poems, the most memorable lines are those that express fierce indignation:

Beating the drums
my poetic voice
proclaimed to all:
those are unstained hands.
Now,
a slap in my face!

Along the same lines, the poet expresses, in another poem titled "By the River", his disappointment at the conflict between Tamil militant groups, resulting in mindless death.

Folks
do not build bridges
with corpses
to cross the river.

It is quite likely that Cheran's refusal to remain tied to any particular stance has given him a range and depth that sets him apart from many other poets.

Cheran's significance as a poet has been both documented and discussed more fully than perhaps any other contemporary Tamil poet. He is also perhaps the best known in India and internationally. Among Sri Lankan scholars, Sivathamby and Sivasegaram have written incisive essays on his poetry, while in Tamil Nadu Sundara Ramaswamy, Jeyamohan, Gnanakoothan, D. Ravikumar and M. Ramasamy, among others, have drawn attention to his work.[vii] Although he started writing in the early 70s, he is some ways the product of a time when the political scene was beginning to change rapidly, and the cultural forms of representation were becoming a crucial part of the transformation. In addition to being deeply concerned about politics and culture, his poetry was meant for a large readership, without necessarily jettisoning a commitment to a noticeable intellectual rigor. To put it differently, the distinctiveness of his poetry lies in his capacity to bring together the traditional and the modern, the lyrical and the intellectual. Even at its most abstract, the poetry retains the tone of oral delivery, while the various tropes insist on a complex train of thought. Cheran's poetry, in addition to being deeply contextual, forces the reader to read carefully and slowly. This could have something to do with his own training in the sciences, or his academic life as a sociologist, but the fact remains that internal logic of his poems compels the reader to pay close attention to the working of language and metaphor.

Cheran began writing consistently at a time when students, particularly undergraduates, were deeply preoccupied with the rapid escalation of political conflict. Poetry was seen as an important way of reaching out to the people, and Cheran himself, having grown up with the notion of poetry as performance, was now able to harness this experience and mold it to the new context. His poetry was both recited and performed in towns and villages. And in these instances, passion and lyricism were as important as intellectual rigor. Cheran's poetry, in its performative aspect, needed to engage with people in a very direct manner. He is among a handful of poets who wrote many poems that were meant to be sung and performed and an equal number of poems that were deeply introspective and intellectually complex. The latter, in particular, are distinctly modernist and do not lend themselves easily to oral delivery. In them a number of graphic and disturbing images, not overtly connected to each other, are put together so that the overall effect on the reader is both diachronic and synchronic. These poems have a distinctly imagist and surreal quality to them. Through a process of defamiliarisation they demonstrate a passionate commitment to political events and a skepticism about the danger of emotional excess.

For those who are familiar with the cultural and political context which form the backdrop to Cheran's poetry, a number of poems remain emphatically specific. A few poems, such as "The Second Sunrise" are intended to draw attention to certain events that are well known to everyone. In that sense, such poems are metonymic. Here the poet assumes the role of chronicler, speaking about a particular event in ways that are new and significant. Many other poems, however, are deliberately ambivalent. For the reader who has extensive knowledge of the political backdrop these poems are about specific places and events. For others, the poems are sufficiently generalized to express the pervasive experience of pain, loss and trauma. It is this capacity to maintain a balance between the specific and the general that has enabled Cheran's poems to remain relevant long after certain events have faded from collective memory. A poem such as "Glass Rain" reverberates at many levels, and while the Western reader and a Tamil reader might respond to the poem in very different ways, the chances are that both will recognize the trauma of entrapment and mass destruction.

Jeyamohan in an essay makes the observation that the poem about the burning of the Jaffna Public Library is among the best that Cheran has written.[viii] It is perhaps more true to say that such poems reflect the distinctiveness of Cheran's poetry and sets it apart from many others. These poems draw attention to a political context that is not always overt, but familiar to those who have some knowledge of the times. Often the references are quite specific to particular moments or events. The poet positions himself as an insider, very much like the informed reader. As the poem progresses, the particular event begins to shed light in very different ways. Layers of meaning begin to accumulate, changing the event through an imagination that moves across time and space. The poem itself becomes increasingly allusive until the specific and the general merge, and a particular moment is both fixed in time and timeless in its deeper meanings. As Jeyamohan implies, this is precisely why a poem about a particular time and place transcends its temporal boundaries to become a major work. There is tremendous irony and pathos in calling the burning of a major library as a kind of sunrise. But the irony is deliberate. To call it a form of sunset would rob the poem of its urgency, resolve, and optimism.

Linking the specific to the general or the metonymic to the metaphoric often entails a number of challenges for the poet. In the first instance, the moment that occasions a particular poem engages the subjectivity of the poet, compelling him to write in ways that draw on certain images. In poems such as "By the River" which might well refer to the conflicts between two militant groups, the cluster of images draw on the landscape, the river, and nature, to emphasize specificity. But such conflicts are also reminiscent of other conflicts that are needlessly destructive, and in order to encapsulate them within the frame of the poem, the imagery becomes very different. Two levels thus coexist in Cheran's poetry, making him both a very local poet concerned with immediate realities and a modernist poet with a broad sweep. Tracking certain patterns of imagery is often a useful way of understanding the thematic links that run through Cheran's work.

Among the recurring tropes in Cheran's corpus, the sea appears time and again in various forms. It is not without significance that his very first poem was titled "Sea" when it appeared in 1975. His most recent collection is titled *Meendum Kadalukku* (Back to the Sea), published, coincidentally, soon after the Tsunami hit South Asia. For an island people, it is hardly surprising that the sea is important in both a literal and metaphoric sense. The sea provides freedom and security; it is a protection against outsiders, but it also alienates and makes people insular and vulnerable. The sea takes on a special significance as it embraces various forms of water – rivers, wells, tears, and so forth. His collected poems, published in 2000, has an equally interesting title: *Nee Ippozhuthu Irangum Aru* (The River You Now Step into), implying the inevitability of change and movement. Writing in the 70s, the sea was benign:

Evenings caressed by the night,
the palmyrah leaves then
lift their heads and sway,
now the waves rise in
the caress of the night
the caress of the night. (*Nee Ippozhuthu Irangum Aaru*, 24)

In the post-1983 phase, the imagery and the diction change:

From this shore to the next,
long, heat-carrying tubes,
run across the bottom;
the water torn apart,
icebergs shattered
the path they create
day and night
ships ply the sea. (*Meendum Kadalukku*, 25)

Between the tragedy of ethnic violence and the sorrow of exile, Cheran finds himself writing a poetry that combines restraint with a deep sense of commitment. In poems such as "Demonic Eyes" the contemporary political scene becomes the occasion for unrestrained satire. It is also multi-faceted satire, looking inward and outward, speaking of the past but foretelling the future. It even invokes the notion of gender without becoming dogmatic in its stance. Cheran often alludes to the demonic and the supernatural to find a trope for the excesses that people face all the time. Often the imagery provides a sense of distance, while the rhythms retain that sense of familiarity. As Sivathamby says quite rightly, 'Cheran's poetry demonstrates how the new generation recognizes, respond to and understands the experiential changes in society.'[ix] Negotiating this change is as much about subject matter as it is about style and language. Often the shift in perspective, the movement from one voice to another may become a strategy for including multiple voices and perspectives. Cheran's struggle as a poet comes from the recognition that tradition is both an asset and an impediment. Working with a literary tradition that goes back to more than twenty centuries often entails drawing from a rich archive of poetic forms and linguistic diversity. If Cheran's poetry has a rich oral dimension it is because Tamil poetry has always incorporated an oral quality. For Cheran it is as important to draw from the past while defamiliarizing his poetry in order to make it both contemporary and original.

Cheran's first collection of poems is titled *Irandavathu Suriya Uthayam* (The Second Dawn). Ironically, the second dawn symbolizes the fire that engulfed the Jaffna Public Library when it was burned down in 1981. Since then, with each book, the title has a story to tell. These stories chart the poet's emotional story through tempestuous times, leading to exile in Canada. The imagination that captures these narratives is often quite startling in its capacity to accommodate the inhuman and the non-human. A severed leg or a demonic goddess can become the subject of his poems, but the language remains both grounded and strange at the same time. The reader is often swept along by the rhythm, the repetitions, the refrains, all of which suggest a certain familiarity between the poet and the reader. And yet the structure of the poem is deliberately allusive, moving across time and space, always implying layers of complex meaning.

In fact, in his critical writing he has advanced the very interesting notion that the social and cultural backdrop of the diaspora needs to be thought of not simply as nostalgia or exile, but as an extension of the *tinai* concept prevalent in Sangam poetry.[x] Inasmuch as the poetics of the Sangam age was dependent on particular aspects of landscape, so does the poetry of diaspora draw on the specificities of an alien landscape and its social practices. His notion of diaspora as self-sufficient space with its own norms and conventions allows for his poetry to acquire that sense of naturalness while being different. Thus a meeting between the poet and a First Nations Elder is both unusual and predictable. Such poems maintain that balance between the unfamiliar and the familiar that is crucial to his poetry. Diaspora has been, for Cheran, a source of empowerment. While the yearning for "home" has not been in any way diminished by distance, diaspora has extended the range of his perception, and shaped the trajectory of his poetry.

Cheran's displacement within the country and in Europe was often the result of escaping the wrath of different players in the political arena. In such circumstances, the poetry remained committed to the particular and the specific. It was hardly possible to be an activist and a poet without invoking the political events of the time. Pathos, outrage, and optimism are all inevitable subjective responses to the constant changes as one scenario gave way to another. Cheran's poems continue to engage us largely because the poems are shaped by an imagination that goes beyond the immediate. The widespread violence of 1983 might be the immediate context of a particular poem, but the I/eye that perceives the carnage focuses on a particular moment that in its insignificance suddenly takes on a human dimension that goes beyond the immediate moment. In a poem such as "Forgetting" the poet records in minute detail moments of horror as people are blown apart, but the most tragic moment is when a pot of rice is shattered, and a woman's children, hiding in the bushes, are denied their food. Understatement is a staple feature of Cheran's poetry. At the most intense moments, the diction gets pared down to essentials. The prose is simple, almost monosyllabic, but retains its powerful impact.

From the time he began writing three decades ago, Cheran has been concerned with the role of the poet in times of upheaval. In poems that were written in times when his own safety was in question, the poet expresses both the trauma of having to live in hiding and also the commitment to survive. Time and again, such poems assert the need for both awareness and distance. These are poems of fear and terror as the language offers a range of imagery that overturns a natural order:

What will happen
when I die and depart?

If it happens to be dawn
the moon will rise.

.....

If it happens to be night
the birds, woken from sleep,
will sing.

In the melody of that song
The feathers of the lapwing will burn.

The poet must survive, and bear witness to the carnage around. Cheran's poetry is always conscious that it is all too easy to be swept away by the horror of the moment. But the poet is also the chronicler of the times and must struggle to preserve a sense of detachment:

Unperturbed
he writes his poem

Something of this uncertainty comes across in many of his self-reflexive poems in which he feels the need to reiterate his commitment to life and to his freedom to criticize. Even in his bleakest poems, there is a determination to live, to express his complex response to the violence around.

let my pyre burn
to shed a tiny light.

From that light
a song will appear.

Ideas of conflict, resistance, subversion, recuperation, fragmentation and dispersal keep appearing in various guises. The more recent poems are, in that sense, no different. But the telling has been always shaped by circumstance. In the aftermath of the violence of 2009, the poems are spare, devoid of profusion of imagery, but powerful nonetheless. The distance between his recent poems and his early poems in the 1970s is quite striking, and they indicate the impressive trajectory of a remarkable body of poetry. Derek Walcott ends his poem titled "Mass Man" with the following stanza:

Upon your penitential morning.
some skull must rub its memory with ashes,
some mind must squat down howling in your dust,
some hand must crawl and recollect your rubbish,
someone must write your poems.[xi]

This is precisely what Cheran has done over a period of three decades.

Notes

1. Ravikumar, ed. *Waking is Another Dream*, New Delhi: Navayana, 2010: 28.
2. For the complete interview, see *Kalachchuvadu* (July-Sept. 99): 11-32..
3. See above. Translation mine.
4. Cheran's publications include *Irandavathu Suriya Uthayam* (1983), *Yaman* (1984), *Kaanal Vari* (1989), *Elumbu Koodukalin Urvalam* (1990), and *Erithu Kondirukkum Neram* (1993). For his collected poems, see, A. Yesurasa R. Cheran, *Nee Ippozhuthu Irangum Aaru* (Nagercoil, Tamil Nadu: Kalachuvadu, 2000). His most recent collection is titled *Meendum Kadalukku* (2005).
5. Preface to *Maranaththul*, p. 11
6. For Sundara Ramaswamy's essay, see *Kalachchuvadu*, 32 (Nov-Dec, 2000): 210-14.
7. See S. Sivasegaram, *Vimarsanagal*, Madras: South Asian Books, 1995, and B. Jeyamohan, *Kaalam* (December, 2008): 24-36.
8. See *Kaalam* (December, 2008): 24-36.
9. See K. Sivathamby, *Tamil Elakkiath Thadam* 1980-2000, Colombo: Moonravathu Manithan, 2000: 101
10. For a detailed discussion, see "Citizens of Many Worlds: Theorizing Tamil DiasporiCity" in History and Imagination: Tamil Culture in the Global Context, ed. R. Cheran, Darshan Ambalavanar and Chelva Kanaganayakam (Toronto: TSAR, 2007): 150-168.
11. Derek Walcott, *Selected Poetry*, London: Heinemann, p. 31.

நீரற்றது கடல்
நிலமற்றது தமிழ்
பேரற்றது உறவு

Parched ocean
silent land
nameless kin

Conflict

எனது நிலம்

சிறகுவலை விரித்த பரவைக் கடல்
மேலே மூச்செறியும் காற்று
கடல் நடுவில்,
கலையும் தலைமயிரை
விரல்களாலழுத்தி நிமிர்கையிலெல்லாம்
கரை தெரிகிறது,
பனைமரமும் இடையிடையே ஓடுகளும்.

அலையும், எஞ்சின் இரையும் பொழுது
சிதறும் துளியும்
ஒன்றரை மணி நேரம்
எப்படி முடிந்ததாம்?

பிறகு, மணல் நிமிர்ந்த வெளி
அதனுள் புதைந்த பனைகள்,
ஒவ்வொன்றும் ஓராள் உயரமெனக்
கன்னி மணல்மீது தலைநீட்டும்
மணலோ,
கண்ணாடி விதையிட்டுச்
சூரியன் போய்க் குடியிருந்த
பொன்னின் துகள்
அதன்கீழ்
இரண்டாயிரம் ஆண்டுகள்
முன்பாக, என் முன்னோர் நடந்த
நிலப்பரப்பு.
ஒரு காலடி ஆனால்
ஓராயிரம் ஆண்டு
எம் வேர் நீண்டுள்ளது.

My Land

A net spread across the shallow waters
the heavy breath of the wind above,
from the middle of the ocean,
fingers pressing down
the unruly hair,
we look up
see the shore,
palmyrah trees, and sporadically
the tiled roofs.

The waves,
the spray and
the roar of engines
ninety minutes
how did they end?

Later, an expanse of sand
the rooted
palmyrah trees,
each the height of a man,
on that virgin sand;
the sand itself,
buried mirrors
where the sun settles;
reflections of gold;
beneath that
two thousand years ago
my ancestors walked
this earth;
one footstep
a thousand years;
our roots are deep.

துயிலாது, இந்த அலைகரையில்
நின்று
விண்மீன் சிதறிக் கடலுள்
விழுகிறதைப் பார்த்திரங்கிய ஒருத்தியின்
அல்லது
தொடுவான் வெளி பிளந்து
கரை சேரும் நாவாய்க்குக்
காத்திருந்த இன்னொருத்தியின்
வெறும் மார்பில் புரண்ட மணி ஒன்றில்
பின்மாலை, அந்திப் பொழுது
புடமிட்ட
தென்னோலை காற்றாடும் வெளியின்
மண் மூடிய சுவடுகளில்,
என்
முன்னோர்
விட்டுப் போயுள்ளார்கள்
எனக்கொரு செய்தி

நூறுநூறாயிரம் தோள்களின்மீது
ஏறி நின்று,
எனது நிலம் என உரத்துச் சொல்கிறேன்.
ஏழு சமுத்திர வெளிகளைத் தாண்டி
அதன் மேல் எழுகிற அலைகளை மீறி
அதனைக் கொண்டு போய்,
எங்கும் ஒலிக்கிறது காற்று

“எனது நிலம்
எனது நிலம்”.

Sleepless, one woman
standing on these shores,
lamenting the stars
falling into the sea;
or another, waiting for
the horizon to split apart,
bring her boat home;
on her bare breasts
trinkets in which, or
in the footprints
now covered by sand
that late evening, with
coconut trees swaying in the wind,
my ancestors
have left a message
for me.

On a hundred thousand shoulders
I stand
This is my land, I shout;
across the seven seas
defying the rising waves
the wind carries
this voice:

My land
My land.

இரண்டாவது சூரிய உதயம்

அன்றைக்குக் காற்றே இல்லை,
அலைகளும் எழாது செத்துப் போயிற்று
கடல்.

மணலில் கால் புதைதல் என
நடந்து வருகையில்
மறுபடியும் ஒரு சூரிய உதயம்.

இம்முறை தெற்கிலே

என்ன நிகழ்ந்தது?
எனது நகரம் எரிக்கப்பட்டது,
எனது மக்கள் முகங்களை இழந்தனர்,
எனது நிலம், எனது காற்று
எல்லாவற்றிலும்
அந்நியப் பதிவு.

கைகளைப் பின்புறம் இறுகக் கட்டி
யாருக்காகக் காத்திருந்தீர்கள்?
முகில்களின்மீது
நெருப்பு,
தன் சேதியை எழுதியாயிற்று
இனியும் யார் காத்துள்ளனர்?

சாம்பல் பூத்த தெருக்களிலிருந்து
எழுந்து வருக.

The Second Sunrise

On that day,
there was no wind;
no rising tide,
even the waves had died.
Sea.

Walking across,
feet sinking in the sand,
again a sunrise.

This sunrise in the South.

What happened?
My town was burned;
my people became faceless;
in my land, my air,
in everything,
the stamp of outsiders.

Hands clasped behind you,
who do you wait for?
On the clouds
fire
has written its tale;
who waits even now?

From the ashen streets,
arise and march.

இரு காலைகளும் ஒரு பின்னிரவும்

இன்றைக்கு, இப்படித்தான்
விடியல் :
இருள் முழுதும் பிரியாது,
ஒளி நிறைந்து விரியாத
ஒரு நேரம்
விழித்தெழுந்து வெளியில் வரக்
கிணற்றடியின் அரசமரக் கிளைகளிலே
குயில் கூவும்
'ஓ' வென்று நிலத்தின் கீழ்
ஆழத்துள் விரிந்திருந்த
கிணறு,
சலனமற்று உறங்கியது
என் மனம் போல.

இன்றைக்கு இப்படித்தான்
விடியல்

நாளைக்கும்,
இப்படித்தான் விடியும்
என்று நினையாதே
பாதி ராத்திரியும் மெதுவாகப்
போனபின்பு, 'கேற்' றடியில்
அடிக்குரலில் ஜீப் வண்டி உறுமும்,
சப்பாத்தொலிகள் தடதடக்கும்.
அதிர்ந்ததென
எம் வீட்டுக் கதவுகளோ
விரிந்து திறந்துகொள்ள,
அப்போதுதான்,
அடுத்தநாள் பரீட்சைக்கு
விரிவுரைக் குறிப்புகள்

Two Mornings and a Late Night

Today, this is how
it dawns:
the night still lingers,
the light's expanse muted,
at this time;
to wake and step out
when the koel sings
from the branch of a well-side tree;
below the earth,
deep and broad,
the well
sleeps peacefully,
like my heart.

Today, this is how
it dawns.

Do not think
it will be such dawn again
tomorrow;
halfway through the night,
at the gate,
the deep growl of the jeep,
the clatter of boots;
with a shudder
the doors of our house
spread open;
then
eyes half closed and tired
having studied
for the test next day,
in that night

விழுங்கிக் களைத்ததில்
விழிகள் மூடிய அந்த இரவிலே
அவர்கள் கூப்பிடுவது கேட்கும்
காதில் ஊளையிடும் காற்று

“எங்கே அவன்” என்று கேட்பார்கள்
கேட்கையிலே
பிழைபட்ட தமிழ் நெஞ்சை நெருட
எழுந்து வரும்

வார்த்தையற்று அதிர்ந்துபோய்
“இல்லை” எனத் தலையாட்ட
இழுத்தெறிவார் ஜீப்பினுள்
நிறுத்தாத எஞ்சின் அப்போதும்
இரைந்தபடி

பிறகு, பிறகென்ன?

காலை. வெறுஞ் சூரியன்.
நிலத்தில் எனக்கு மேல்
புல்.

சிலவேளை வீடுவந்து
கதவு திறப்பதற்காய் குரல் காட்டி
திறக்க முன்பு
இருமிச் சளி உமிழ முகம் திருப்ப
உள்ளிருந்தும்
அம்மா இருமும் ஒலி கேட்கும்.

கதவு திறப்பதற்காய்க் காத்திருந்தேன்
வெளியுலகம்
இப்போதும் முன்போல
அடங்கி இருக்கிறது

we hear "their" call;
the howling wind
in our ears.
"Where he is?" they ask,
their broken Tamil
pierces the heart.

Speechless
stunned,
as we shake our heads
flung into the jeep
the running engine
still growling.

What then?
It is life
as usual.

The morning sun
on bare earth
above me
grass.

Sometimes coming home
wanting to announce
before opening the door,
turning aside
to hawk and spit,
from inside
the sound of amma's cough.

I waited
to open the door.
The world outside
as before
lay calm.

யமன்

காற்று வீசவும்
அஞ்சும் ஓர் இரவில்
நட்சத்திரங்களுக்கிடையே இருக்கிற
அமைதியின் அர்த்தம் என்ன
என்று
நான் திகைத்த ஓர் கணம்,

கதவருகே யாருடைய நிழல் அது?

நான் அறியேன்,
அவர்களும் அறியார்.
உணர்வதன் முன்பு
அதுவும் நிகழ்ந்தது

மரணம்.

காரணம் அற்றது,
நியாயம் அற்றது.
கோட்பாடுகளும் விழுமியங்களும்
அவ்வவ்விடத்தே உறைந்துபோக
முடிவிலா அமைதி.

மூடப்பட்ட கதவு முகப்பில்,
இருளில்,
திசை தெரியாது
மோதி மோதிச் செட்டையடிக்கிற
புறாக்களை.

தாங்கும் வலுவை என்
இதயம் இழந்தது.

Yaman

The wind falters
as fear
fills the night;
I gasp
at the stillness
between the stars.

Whose shadow lurks by the door?

I wouldn't know,
nor would they;
it happened
swiftly.

Death.

No reason
no justice
values and virtues
freeze where they stand
in the oppressive silence.

In the dark
lost in flight
pigeons
pound and pound again
against the door;

my resolve to endure
slips.

இளைய வயதில்
உலகை வெறுத்தா

நிறங்களை உதிர்த்தன,
வண்ணத்துப் பூச்சிகள்?

புழுதி படாது
பொன் இதழ் விரிந்த
சூரியகாந்தியாய்,
நீர் தொடச்
சூரிய இதழ்கள் விரியும்
தாமரைக் கதிராய்,
நட்சத்திரங்களாய்
மறுபடி அவை பிறக்கும்.

அதுவரை,
பொய்கைக் கரையில்
அலைகளைப் பார்த்திரு!

Do the butterflies
disdaining life
shed their colors
in the prime of youth?

As sunflowers
their golden petals
untouched by dust,
lotus flowers
that bloom at the
touch of water;
as stars,
they will be
born again;

until then
at the edge of the lake,
stare at the waves.

எல்லாவற்றையும் மறந்துவிடலாம்

எல்லாவற்றையும் மறந்துவிடலாம்
இந்தப் பாழும் உயிரை
அநாதரவாக இழப்பதை வெறுத்து
ஒருகணப் பொறியில் தெறித்த
நம்பிக்கையோடு
காலி வீதியில்
திசைகளும், திசைகளோடு இதயமும்
குலுங்க விரைந்தபோது,

கவிழ்க்கப்பட்டு எரிந்த காரில்
வெளியே தெரிந்த தொடை எலும்பை,
ஆகாயத்திற்கும் பூமிக்குமிடையில்
எங்கோ ஒரு புள்ளியில் நிலைத்து
இறுகிப்போன ஒரு விழியை,
விழியே இல்லாமல், விழியின் குழிக்குள்
உறைந்திருந்த குருதியை,
'டிக்மண்ட்ஸ்' ரோட்டில்
தலைக் கறுப்புகளுக்குப் பதில்
இரத்தச் சிவப்பில் பிளந்து கிடந்த
ஆறு மனிதர்களை,
தீயில் கருகத் தவறிய
ஒரு சேலைத் துண்டை,
துணையிழந்து,
மணிக்கூடும் இல்லாமல்
தனித்துப்போய்க் கிடந்த
ஒரு இடது கையை,
எரிந்துகொண்டிருக்கும் வீட்டிலிருந்து
தொட்டில் ஒன்றைச்
சுமக்க முடியாமல் சுமந்துபோன
ஒரு சிங்களக் கர்ப்பிணிப் பெண்ணை

Forgetting

We can forget all;
spurning the loss
of this miserable life,
with the confidence
sparked in a moment;
along Galle Road,
we race
with pounding hearts;

jutting from the burning car,
a thigh bone;
fixed on a spot
between the earth and sky
a staring eye;
no eye, but the socket
filled with blood,
on Dickman's Road;
instead of black heads
bloodied remants
of six men;
a piece of cloth
escaping the fire,
severed,
without a watch
a lonely left arm;
from the burning house
carrying the weight
of a cradle
a pregnant Sinhalese woman,

all these,
all these can be forgotten.

எல்லாவற்றையும்,
எல்லாவற்றையுமே மறந்துவிடலாம்.
ஆனால்
உன் குழந்தைகளை ஒளித்துவைத்த
தேயிலைச் செடிகளின் மேல்
முகில்களும் இறங்கி மறைத்த
அந்தப் பின்மாலையில்
நீண்ட நாட்களுக்குப் பிறகு கிடைத்த
கொஞ்ச அரிசியைப் பானையிலிட்டுச்
சோறு பொங்கும் என்று
ஒளிந்தபடி காத்திருந்தபோது
பிடுங்கி எறிபட்ட என் பெண்ணே,
உடைந்த பானையையும்
நிலத்தில் சிதறி
உலர்ந்த சோற்றையும்
நான் எப்படி மறக்க?

But
that late evening
when the clouds
descended to conceal
the tea bushes
where you hid your children,
when after so long
with the little rice
in the pot
you waited, hiding
for the rice to cook,
you were shattered.
How can I forget,
the broken pot,
the scattered rice?

பகல் பொழுதின் மரணம்

ஒவ்வொரு நாளும்
இரவு,
எல்லோரும் படுத்த பிற்பாடு
நாய்களின் அரவம் குன்றி,
நட்சத்திரங்கள் வெறும் வானுடன்
தனித்த போது
தூங்கப் போவேன்.

சனங்கள் நெருங்கிய
சந்தடியில்
ஓடவும் முடியாது,
இருக்கவும் தெரியாது
மூச்சு வாங்கிச் சரிகிறதான
ஒரு கனவில்
பாதி இரவில்
விழிப்பு வரும்.

ஓரோர் சமயம்
கடலும், நதியும் மஞ்சளாகக்
கார்த்திகைப் பூக்கள்
புறம் புறம் விரிய
நடத்தலும் வரும்

காலையில் எழுந்ததும்
கைகள் ஒருபுறம்
கால் ஒரு திசையில்
முகமும்தான் எங்கோ
சிதறிக் கிடக்கும்.

அனைத்தையும் பொருத்தி
நிமிர்ந்து வந்து
எனது பகலை
உன்னிடம் விற்கிறேன்.

Death of a Day

Every day
in the night
when all sleep
and dogs cease to bark,
only the stars now alone
with the sky,
I go to sleep.

In a crowded street,
unable to run,
not knowing how to sit,
breathless and faltering;
such a dream
halfway through the night,
I wake up.

Sometimes
the sea and river turn yellow
and November flowers
unfold;
I dream of walking.

I wake in the morning
my hands in one place
legs in another,
even my face
scattered elsewhere.

I gather and connect them,
stand upright
and my day
I sell to you.

ராணுவ முகாமிலிருந்து கடிதங்கள்

அன்பே நந்தா,

இன்று காலைதான் வந்துசேர்ந்தோம்.
பிரச்சினை இல்லை.
மடியில்
ரை∴பிளை இறுகப் பற்றியிருந்ததில்
தூக்கமுமில்லை.
கனவுகள்,
மிகவும் பயங்கரம்
திடீரென விழிப்பு.

ரயில் நிலையத்தில்
நீயும் மாமியும் அழுத அழுகையில்
நானுமே பயந்தேன்.
ஆனால்,
அனைவரும் எனக்குச் சொன்னதுபோல
வடக்கு
அப்படி ஒன்றும் பயங்கரமாகத்
தெரியவில்லை.
எங்கும் போலவே
கடைகள், தெருக்கள்,
வாகன நெரிசல்.
மனிதர்கள்தான் எமைப் பார்ப்பதேயில்லை.
தற்செயலாகப் பார்க்கிறபோதும்
அவர்கள் எல்லோரது கண்களினூடும்
ஏதோ ஒன்று

இனம் புரியாத ஓர் உணர்வு
என்னவாயிருக்கும் அது
என எனக்குப் புரியவே இல்லை.

Letters From an Army Camp

Dear Nanda:

arrived this morning,
no problems;
I could hardly sleep,
while gripping the rifle
on my lap;
horrible dreams,
I kept waking
with a shudder.

You and your mother
wept bitterly
at the station;
I too was scared,
but
what I was told
about the North
was not true;
as in every place,
shops, streets
throng of vehicles,
but people avert their eyes,
if they happen to look
I see in their eyes
something,

a flicker,
its meaning
I don't understand.

நாங்கள் தனித் தனியாகச்
செல்வது இயலாது என்பதை
நீ அறிவாய் அல்லவா?
இரண்டு கவச வாகனங்கள்,
வேறு ஜீப்புகள் இரண்டு,
அல்லது மூன்று,
ட்ரக் ஒன்று
இவற்றில் குறைந்தது
ஐம்பது பேராவது ஒன்றாய்ச் செல்வோம்.
அது,
உண்மையிலேயே ஒரு
அணிவகுப்புத்தான்
சுதந்திர தின விழாவில்
பார்த்திருப்பாயே
அப்படித்தான்.
ஆனால் ஒரேயொரு வித்தியாசம் :
சுதந்திர தினத்து அணிவகுப்பில்
எங்களுக்கு சுதந்திரம் இருந்தது
துப்பாக்கிகளுக்கு குண்டுகள் இல்லை.
இங்கோ,
துப்பாக்கிகளுக்கு வேண்டுமான அளவு
குண்டுகள்,
ஆனால், சுதந்திரம் இல்லை

2
இன்று முழுவதும் மிகுந்த அலைச்சல்
பனை மரங்களுடாக வளைந்து வளைந்து
செல்லும் தெருக்களில்
(அவை மிக மோசம்)
கவச வாகனம் குலுங்கக் குலுங்க
இடுப்பு எலும்பெல்லாம்
பிறகு ஒரே வலி.

மத்தியானம்
வயல்வெளிகளுக்கு நடுவிலிருந்த

You know
we cannot
travel by ourselves;
two armored vehicles
two jeeps or
three;
a truck
fifty of us at least
travel together
that is really a parade;
you would have seen
on independence day
just like that;
one difference,
in that parade
we were free
our guns empty,
now,
we have bullets
are no longer free.

2

Today was exhausting,
on the winding road
(they are terrible)
between the palmyrah trees
the armored vehicles jolting
the bones in my back
hurt so much.

Midday,
in a village
among the fields
we shot

ஒரு கிராமத்தில்
மூன்று கொழுத்த ஆடுகள் சுட்டோம்.
இளைஞர்கள் இல்லை,
பெண்கள் ஓடி ஒளிந்துகொண்டார்கள்.
முகாமுக்கு மீள்கிற பாதிவழியில்
மேஜருக்குரிய சிகரெட் வாங்க
மறந்துபோனதை
ஒருவன் ஞாபகப்படுத்தவும்,
பிறகென்ன?
அணிவகுப்பாக அவ்வளவு பேரும்
நகருக்குத் திரும்ப நேர்ந்தது

3

இன்று,
எதிரிவீரவும், சந்திரசிறியும்
மூன்று தமிழரைச் சுட்டுக் கொன்றனர்.
'நெருக்கடி மிகுந்த தெருவில்
திடீரென இவர்கள் ஓடிச் சென்றதால்,
கலவரமுற்றுச் சுட்டுவிட்டேன்'

என்று சந்திர சொன்னான், பிறகு,
விசாரணையின்றியே
இரண்டு பேரையும்
கொழும்புக்கு அனுப்பினர்
இடமாற்றம்தான்.
(கொடுத்து வைத்தவர்கள்)

யாரையாவது சுட்டால்
அல்லது
சனங்கள் மீது தாக்குதல் நிகழ்த்தினால்
வீடுகளைப் பற்றவைத்தால்
உடனடியாக மாற்றம் கிடைக்கிறது (?)

three fat goats;
no young men around,
the women ran and hid;
halfway on our return,
someone remembered
we hadn't bought
cigarettes
for the Major.
What then,
the entire convoy
now wound its way
back to the city.

3

Today
Edirweera and Chandrasiri
shot and killed three Tamils.
"In a crowded street
suddenly they ran,
confused, I shot them,"
explained Chandra.
Later,
no inquiry
both sent to Colombo
transferred
(lucky ones).

Shoot someone
attack the public
set fire to homes
an immediate transfer.

நேற்றும் ஐந்து பேர்
உடனடியாக மாற்றம்பெற்றனர்.
நான் வந்ததிலிருந்து
மொத்தமாக ஐம்பது பேராவது
திரும்பி விட்டனர்,
எப்போது எனக்கு மாற்றம் வருமோ
நான் அறியேன்.

4

இன்றும் புதிதாக நூறு பேர்
எங்கள் முகாமுக்கு வந்தனர்
சின்னப் பயல்கள்,
மீசைகூட அரும்புதான்.
இயந்திரத் துவக்கை இயக்குவதிலோ
திறமையும் குறைவு...

இப்போதெல்லாம்
பகலில் அலைந்து திரிந்த பின்னரும்
இரவில் தூக்கம் பிடிப்பதேயில்லை.
நீண்ட நாளாயிற்று
உன்னை நேரே பார்த்து.
விடுமுறை என்பது நினைக்கவே
இயலாதது...

5

நேற்று இரவு
எமது பிரிவின் பதின்மூன்றுபேரை
'அவர்கள்' கொன்றனர்
குறி பிசகாத குண்டுவெடிப்பின் பின்
சுற்றி வளைத்தன இயந்திரத் துவக்குகள்.
நாங்கள்
எவருமே இதனை எதிர்பார்க்கவில்லை.

Yesterday,
five were transferred,
since I arrived
fifty at least

have returned;
when would I be
transferred,
I don't know.

4

Today one hundred
soldiers
joined our camp.
Youngsters,
hardly a moustache,
not even trained
to handle machine guns.

Now
even after roaming
during the day,
the night brings
no sleep.
So long
since I saw you,
but asking for leave
unthinkable.

5

Last night
"they" killed
thirteen of us;
with deadly accuracy,
a bomb exploded
followed by machine guns
that surrounded us;
no one expected this;

தலைமை முகாமுடன் வானொலித் தொடர்பு
இடையறாமல் இருந்தும்,
இருட்டினுள் யமனின்
இருப்பை மீற
ஒன்றுமே இயலாது போயிருக்க வேண்டும்.

அடுத்தநாட் காலை
எந்தத் தெருவிலும் சனங்கள் இல்லை,
கடைகள் இல்லை.
அர்த்தம் தெரியாமல் ஓர் அமைதி
என்ன தேசம் இது?

இப்போதெல்லாம்
இரவு மிகவும் கொடூரம் மிக்கது.
நிலவொளி படர்கையில்
நிழல்கள் அசைவதும்
பெயர் தெரியாத பறவைகள்
திடீரென அலறுவதும்
பகல் வரும்வரையில் நரகம்தான்.

அப்புறம்,
உடனடியாக மாற்றம் கேட்ட
எமது பிரிவு நேற்றுத் தெருவில்
இறங்கிற்று
எத்தனை பேரைச் சுட்டுத் தீர்த்தது
என்ற விபரம் சரியாகத் தெரியாது.
ஐம்பது அல்லது அறுபது என்று
மேஜர் நினைக்கிறார்.

6

அன்பே நந்தா
ஒரு வழியாக எல்லாம் முடிந்தது
நாளை எனக்கு இடமாற்றம்

in spite of constant
radio contact
with the main camp
no escape
as Yaman descended
in the night.

The next morning
no one on the streets
no shops;
a strange silence,
what is this land?

Now
the nights are cruel,
as moonlight spreads
shadows move
suddenly,
strange birds screech,
hell until dawn.

Later
having asked for
immediate transfer,
our division
took to the streets;
how many were killed
we are not sure
fifty or sixty
Major says.

6

Dear Nanda
finally it ended;
tomorrow my transfer,

கடவுளுக்கு நன்றி.
இன்று கடைசித் தடவையாக
நகருக்குச் சென்றேன்
அப்படி ஒன்றும் பயங்கரமாகத்
தெரியவில்லை.
முன்பு போலவே கடைகள், தெருக்கள்
ஆனால், மனிதர்கள்தான்
முன்பு போலவும்
எம்மைப் பார்ப்பதேயில்லை.

thank God.
Today I went
for the last time
to the city;
nothing terrible,
as before, shops and streets
the people
as before,
avert their eyes.

பிசாசுக் கவிதை

இரு புறமும் துப்பாக்கி
நடுவில் நான்
அப்பாவிப் பொதுமகன்
என்பேர்.

ஊரில்லை எனக்கு,
முன்பு இருந்தது
இப்போ தொலைந்துவிட்டது.
(புண்ணிய பாரதத்துக்கு நன்றி!)

இரு புறமும் துப்பாக்கி
நடுவில் நான்
எரிகின்ற நெருப்புக்கும்
நடுவில்தான்.

அவன் ‘இரு’ என்றால்
இவன் ‘எழும்பு’ என்பான்.
இவன் ‘போ’ என்றால்
அவன் ‘வா’ என்பான்.

அவன் ‘இற’ என்றான்.
இவன் ‘இரு’ என்றான்.
அவன் உடலைக் கொன்றான்.
இவன் ஆத்மாவைக் கொன்றான்.

இப்போ நான்
பிசாசானேன்.

The Ghost's Song

Guns on both sides
me in the middle
an innocent commoner
that is my name.

I have no city
I did;
now it is gone
(thanks to holy India!).

Guns on both sides
me in the middle;
a burning fire
me in the middle.

He says "sit"
the other says "stand";
he says "go"
the other says "come."

He said "die"
another said "live";
he slew the body
another killed the soul.

And I became
a ghost.

எலும்புக்கூடுகளின் ஊர்வலம்

அவனது கனவுகள்
சாதாரணமானவை
யாழ்ப்பாண மத்தியதர வர்க்கத்துப்
பனங்கொட்டைக் கனவுகள்

பனங்கொட்டை முளைத்து வளர்ந்து
வடலி,
பின் நெடுத்துப் பெரு வடலியாய்ப்
பனையாகப்
பொறுமையாய் ஆண்டுகள்
இருபது சேரும்,
உறுதியாய் வளரும்
ஒரே மாதிரி.

அதுவரை
காத்திருத்தல் ஒரு யோகம்.

அவனும் விடிய விடியப் படிப்பு
அவன் தூங்கும்வரை
அம்மாவும் விழிப்பு
தேநீர் போடத் தட்டிக் கொடுக்க
இரவின் பிடி மீறத் துணையாக.

அம்மாவுக்கு முடியாதென்றால்
அக்கா அல்லது சின்னவள்

பொறுமையாய் ஆண்டுகள் சேரும்

மருத்துவம், பொறியியல், கணக்கியல்
மும்மூர்த்திகள்
இப்போ புதிதாய்க் 'கொம்பியூட்டர்'
படிப்பும்
மும்மூர்த்திகளுடன் துர்க்கா தேவியின்
புதிய எழுச்சி.

A Procession of Skeletons

His dreams
are ordinary;
the palmyrah dreams
of the Jaffna middle class.

The palmyrah seed grows;
becomes a fence,
then grows further,
a tree and a larger fence;
it survives patiently;
twenty years
it grows firmly
unchanging.

Until then, waiting
a patient sacrifice.

He studies
late into the night
until he sleeps,
his mother is awake,
to nudge, to offer tea
to unclasp the hold of night.

If mother cannot,
then the sister
older or younger.

The years accumulate.

Medicine, engineering, commerce
the triumvirate;
now add computers,
an additional deity
to the three gods.

ஒரு வகையில்
பனையும் இந்தப் படிப்பும் வலியன
வல்லன் வாழும் ஆளும்
அல்லன தேயும் மாளும்
டார்வினுக்கு நன்றி
இது இயற்கை விஞ்ஞானத்தோடு
போகட்டும்
சமூகத்துக்கல்ல.

ஆனால் பனை மரங்களுக்குச் சடைக்கத்
தெரியாது
அவற்றுக்கு உயிரூட்ட
இரவும் நிலவும் காற்றும்
வேண்டும்
சில வேளைகளில் கூடவே
மெல்லிய தொனியில் சங்கீதமும்
வேண்டும்

இல்லையெனில் உலர்ந்து
போகாதோ வாழ்வு?

அவனது கனவுகள் சாதாரணமானவை
அவற்றுக்கும் சடைக்கத் தெரியாது.

ஒரு நாள்
அவனது கனவுகள் உருமாற்றம் பெற்றன

அவற்றில்
எலும்புக் கூடுகள் ஊர்வலமாகப் போயின
ஆண் எலும்புக் கூடுகள்
பெண் எலும்புக் கூடுகள்
சிறுவர் சிறுமிகளின் எலும்புக் கூடுகள்
குழந்தையைக் கையில் தாங்கிய
எலும்புக் கூடுகள்
இளைய எலும்புக் கூடுகள்

In some ways
the palmyrahs and the studies
are sturdy.
The survival of the fittest
the death of the weakest,
thanks to Darwin;
let this bolster
science,
not society.

But
the palymyrah does not
know to thrive;
to give it nourishment,
the air, the night, the moon
sometimes even
gentle music
are needed.

If not for these
would life not waste away?

His dreams are ordinary;
to flourish,
they do not know.

One day
his dreams were transformed.

In those,
a procession of
skeletons
male skeletons
female skeletons
skeletons of kids
skeletons carrying babies
young skeletons,
old skeletons

முதிய எலும்புக் கூடுகள்
கைகளற்றவையும்கூட

ஒரே திசையை நோக்கியபடி
உறைந்து போயிருந்த
அவற்றின் கட்குழிகளிலிருந்து
கண்ணீரும் இரத்தமும்
ஓடிக் கொண்டிருந்தன

ஆயிரக் கணக்கில்
அணியணியாக எலும்புக் கூடுகள்...
அவற்றின்மீது
வெறுப்புமிழும் விழி நிமிர்த்தித்
துப்பாக்கிப் பிரயோகம் செய்தனர்
ராணுவத்தினர்.

ஒரு புறம்
தலைப்பாகை அணிந்திருந்த ராணுவம்
நிஜாம் பாக்கும்
கடலை எண்ணெயும்
நெய்யும்
துண்டு பீடியும் சேர்ந்து
அவலட்சணமாக மணக்கும் ராணுவத்தினர்
இன்னும்
கறுப்பு நிறத்தில் தலைக்குத்
துண்டு கட்டியிருந்தவர்களும்...

மறு புறம்
மினுக்கிய உடையும் மிடுக்கும் மிளிர
மினுங்கும் யப்பானிய வாகனங்களில்
இருந்த ராணுவத்தினர்

இன்னொரு புறமோ
துப்பாக்கியின் திசையை
மாற்றிக்கொண்டுவிட்ட
உள்ளூர் ராணுவம்

even without arms
eyes fixed,
in the same direction
from frozen sockets
streams of blood and tears.

Thousands of them
skeletons in line;
on them
eyes filled with hate
the soldiers
used their guns.

On one side
turbaned soldiers,
the stench of Nijam arecanut
peanut oil
ghee
a half-smoked beedi,
surrounding them;
also,
those with black scarves
around their heads.

On the other
washed clothes and looking trim
in shining Japanese vehicles
soldiers.

Yet another side,
the local army
their guns
now turned elsewhere.

குண்டுகள்
எலும்புக் கூடுகளைத்
துளைத்துக்கொண்டு
நீண்ட தூரம் சென்றன
செல்லத்
தொலைவிலிருந்தும் தோன்ற ஆரம்பித்தன
எலும்புக் கூடுகள்

குண்டுகளை மீறி
கவச வாகனங்களை மிதித்து
அலறி ஓட ஆரம்பித்த
ராணுவத்தினர் மீதாக
ஒவ்வொரடியாக எடுத்து வைத்து
நடந்து போயின எலும்புக் கூடுகள்
அவற்றின் அணியோ
முடிவற்றுத் தெரிகிறது பயங்கரமாக.

கனவின் இடையில் விழித்தவன்
செயின் ஆற்றங்கரையிலும்
வூப்பெற்றால் நகரத்துத்
தொங்கு பாலத்தின் கீழும்
தொறன்ரோ உறைபனித் திரளுக்கு
நடுவிலும்
துண்டுகளாக வீசப்பட்டிருப்தை உணர்ந்தான்.

விழிப்பிலும் கேட்டுக்கொண்டிருக்கிறது
எலும்புக் கூடுகளின்
படையணி ஒலி.

Bullets
pierced the skeletons
and went afar.
Despite the distance to travel,
the skeletons
began to emerge;
defying the bullets
trampling the tanks
stepping on
the scattering soldiers,
they walked,
their procession unending,
fearsome.

Having woken from the dream,
he realized that the scattered pieces
lay on the banks of the Seine,
under the sky track of Wuppertal,
in the snowy terrain
of Toronto.

Now awake,
he still hears
the sound of marching
skeletons

பேய் விழி

கனவற்ற நெடுந்தூக்கத்திலிருந்து
விழித்தெழுந்தாள்:
மாலை மூன்று மணி

பாதி உலகம் தெரியும்

பணிய மறுத்த காதலனை
எட்டி உதைத்த போது
தவறி விழுந்த மதுக் கலசம்
காலடியில் தலை கீழாய்க் கிடக்கிறது

மூடி மூடி மறைத்தாலும்
வேரில் துளிர் விடும் நரை மயிருக்கு
ஒரு இளிவரல் சிரிப்பைப்
பரிசாகத் தருகிறாள்

கொட்டாவி விட்டபோது
திரைச் சேலை விலகிப் பறக்க
ஒளி நுழைகிறது
ஒரு நொடி.

மறுபடி இருள்
அவள் பேய்விழி துலங்கும்
காலடி தளரும்
கைவிரல் நடுங்கும்

காலையிலிருந்து காத்துக் கிடந்த
அமைச்சர்களின் கைத்தொலைபேசிகள்
இறந்து போக
வெறுமையில் குமைகிறது
ஆலோசனை மண்டபம்

Demonic Eyes

She wakes
from a dreamless slumber;
three pm.

Half the world she sees.

A goblet that fell
as she kicked
the defiant lover
lies upturned on the floor.

Sardonic, she smiles
observing
the sprouting grey hair
that refuses to be dyed.

As she yawns
the clothes slip
for just a moment
a sliver of light enters.

Darkness again,
her demonic lids droop
her legs falter
her fingers shake.

The cell phones
of ministers waiting from dawn
now silent,
emptiness looms in
the advisory hall.

இருக்கவும் முடியாது
பொறுமை இழந்து
விலகவும் முடியாத கையறு நிலை
ஏவல் சிறுக்கருக்கு அதுவே சொர்க்கம்

வருகிறாள்.
கிறக்கம் விலகி இருந்தாலும்
இருள் விலகாத விழியாள்
'அவளுடைய சேலைச் சரசரப்பில்
பூக்களும் நிலையிழந்தன'
எனப் பாடல் இசைத்தோர்
புலம் பெயர்ந்து ஒதுங்குகிறார்கள்

அவளைத் தேவதை என்றவர்களின்
வார்த்தைகள்
கழிவறையை நிறைக்கின்றன
அப்பனும் அம்மையும்
பாட்டனும் பூட்டியும் ஊட்டிய
வம்சாவழிச் செருக்குடன்
கொடூர அணிநடைப் படையொலி எழுப்பும்
அவள் கால்களைத் தொடர்ந்து
கால்களை இழந்த படைத் தலைவன்
வருகிறான்.

"உன்னால் முடியுமா?
கொன்றொழிப்பில் உச்சம் எட்டினேன்!"
என்ற அவள் வார்த்தைகளை
எதிர்க்க முடியாமல்
உள்ளாடைகளுக்குள் முகம் புதைக்கிறார்கள்
முன்னைய தலைவர்கள்

நாடும் வீடும் நானிலம் அனைத்தும்
தன்னை மட்டுமே மாய அழகுடன்
பிரதிபலிக்கின்ற ஒரு பெரும் நிலைக் கண்ணாடி
என்கிற சித்தப் பிரமை
அவளுக்கு

They can neither wait
nor, tired of waiting,
leave, a dilemma
that is the sycophant's reward.

She comes;
drunk no more,
but the eyes remain clouded;
those who sang
"Even the flowers swooned
at the rustle of her dress"
now discreetly move away.

The words
that described her as goddess
now fill those sewage pits;
the arrogance fed
by her father and mother,
by the grandparents,
echoing in the harsh
steps of her feet;
followed by her captain
who has no legs himself.

"Can you match
the scale of my destruction?"
Unable to oppose
her words,
the former leaders
now hide their faces.

Home, land, and country
a massive mirror reflecting
none but her beauty –
a madness
hers.

முலை திருகி எறிய
எரிந்து விடும் நாடு
என்கிற அச்சத்தில்
கிழக்கிலும் வடக்கிலும் பெண்களின் முலைகளை
வெடி வைத்துத் தகர்த்து விடுகிறாள்
அவள்.

நகைச்சுவையை அல்ல
குருதியையே திருப்பித் தரும் வரலாற்றின்
கொடூர நாயகி
சிரித்தால் தெறிப்பது அவலம்
விழித்தால் விளைவது துயரம்
நடந்தால் கிடைப்பது நரகம்!

A breast wrenched and flung
can burn a city;
fearing the worst,
breasts of women, in the North and East
she explodes
and destroys.

The demon goddess
of a history that repeats
not laughter but blood itself;
she laughs, scattering pain
she glares, causing grief
she walks, creating hell!

கொலைக் கலைஞர்

மனிதர்களின் கைகளையும் கால்களையும்
தலைகளையும் துண்டித்துக் கொண்டிருந்த போது
இவனை முதன் முதலில் கண்டேன்

"என்ன செய்கிறாய்?" என்று அலறினேன்
பீதியில் முற்றாக வெளிவர மறுத்தது
என் குரல்.

"மிரளாதே. இந்த அழகிய உடல்களுக்குப்
பொருந்தாத உறுப்புகள் இவை.
புதியவற்றைப் பொருத்தவே
இவற்றைத் துண்டாடுகிறேன்
இப்போது தெரியாது என் ரூபம்
பொறுத்திரு ஒரு தலைமுறைக்கு
பிறக்கும் ஒரு புது அழகு"
என்று இவன் சொல்லி முடிக்கும் முன்பே
மனிதர்கள் வரிசையாக
இவனிடம் வருகிறார்கள்
இவன் துண்டாடுகிறான்

இவனது பெருவாளின் கூர்மை
பரிதிச் சுடரின் பொறிகளில் மோதிப்
பேரொளி கிளப்புகிறது

இவனது கைவீச்சில் மனிதருக்கு வசப்படாத
துரிதமும் நளினமும்
பிரிபடா முழுமையாய் இணைக்கின்றன

நெடுங்காட்டுள்
நுனிவிரலில்
நூறாண்டு தவமிருந்து

The Assassin as Artist

People, arms, legs, and
heads were being severed, when
I first met him.

"What are you doing" I splutter,
panic-stricken, my voice hardly
audible.

"Don't be horrified. These limbs
Don't fit these beautiful bodies.
I am chopping them off
to refit new ones.
You cannot see what I am made of,
wait for another decade
a new beauty will be born."
He has barely finished speaking
when people line up
to see him;
he continues to mutilate.

The sharp edge of mighty sword
touched by the rays of the sun
sparkle brightly.

In the swing of his arm, a rarely matched
speed and beauty
come together.

In the dense forest
standing on his toe, praying
for a hundred years
gets this strength.

பெற்ற உடல்
பிளந்தெறியும் போதும் சாந்தம் குடியிருக்கும்
முகபாவம் அவனுக்கு
நிகழ்கால அவலங்களுள் சிக்குண்டிராத
ஒரு முனிவனின் மனோநிலை

இவனது இதயத்துள்
சிலந்தி வலையாகப் படர்ந்திருக்கிறது

இவன் வெட்டியான் அல்லன்
கொலைக் கலைஞன்.

2

அவனுடைய முகம் இப்போது
மறந்து போய்விட்டது எனக்கு
அதில் எப்போதாவது கண்கள் இருந்த
ஞாபகமும் எனக்கு இல்லை
சுவரொட்டிகளிலும் வீட்டின் வரவேற்புக்
கூடங்களிலும் அலுவலகங்களில்
அதிகாரிகளின் பழங்கதிரைகளுக்குப்
பின் சுவரிலும்
கம்பீரமாகக் காட்சி தருகின்றது
அவன் முகம் என்று சொல்கிறார்கள்

ஆனால்
என்ன அநியாயமோ தெரியாது
நான் பார்க்கிற போதெல்லாம்
அவனுடைய படத்தில் முகம்
அழிந்து போகிறது

களங்கமற்ற மனதுடன்
அவனுக்காகத் தன்னுடைய உயிரைத் தருகிற
ஒவ்வொருவருக்கும்

A disposition of calm
even as he destroys
detached from the present
the poise of a saint

spreads across his heart
like a spider's web.

He is not a destroyer
he is the assassin as artist.

2

Now I hardly remember
his face.
I do not know if there were
eyes on that face.
On billboards and in living rooms
in offices on walls behind
old chairs
in all majesty, they say
his face appears.

I cannot fathom
why
when I look, the face
disappears.

For each one, who
with unsullied innocence
gives a life
he offers a gift:
a coffin.

அவன் ஒரு சவப்பெட்டியைப் பரிசாகத் தருகிறான்
புதைத்த பிற்பாடு
அசிங்கமான வண்ணங்களில்
அவர்களுடைய முகங்களைத் தீட்டி
மேற்குக் கரையிலும் காஸாத் தெருமுனையிலும்
காட்சிக்கு வைக்கிறார்கள்
அவனது மெய்ச் சீடர்கள்

இறப்பு என்பது இன்னொரு உலகத்தின்
புதுவாழ்வு என்ற கோலாகலம்

அச்சமும் அலங்காரமும் மேற்பூச்சும்
கண்ணீரை அழித்து விடுகின்றன

இறப்பே அழகானது
இறப்பே இருப்பாயிற்று.

3
இப்போது
புகழ் மிக்க வீரஞ் செறிந்த
இறப்பு
வாழ்க்கையை விடாப் பிடியாகத் தாக்குகிறது

தெருப் புழுதியில் வீசி எறியப்பட்ட
பழங்காகிதமாக வாழ்க்கை தோற்றுப் போகிறது
என்றாலும்
என்னை விட்டு விடுங்கள்
இறப்பு எல்லோருக்குமே
நிச்சயம் என்றாலும்
இறுதித்துளிவரை வாழ்வை ருசித்துக்
கடைசி ஆசையையும் மதுக் கிண்ணத்துள்
வார்த்து
இரும்புச் சுவர்களை ஊடறுத்துத்
தூதனுப்புகிற ஒரு “கோழை” யாய்

When they are buried
in gaudy colours
their faces painted
in West Bank and
on the streets of Gaza
they are displayed
by his disciples.

Death is only the beginning of a
glorious life elsewhere.

Fear, festivity and makeup
wipe away the tears.

Death is beauty,
death is a way of life.

3
Now
a glorious and valiant
death
unleashes a relentless attack on life.

Life, an old page on a dusty street,
now vanquished;
yet
leave me alone;
while it is certain
that all must die
let me savor life to the last drop
my last wish poured into
a cup of wine;
I will survive,
a 'coward' sending messages
through iron walls.

இருந்து விட்டுப் போகிறேன்
துண்டாடும் கொண்டாட்டத்தில்
எனது குரல் அமிழ்ந்து
போகாமல் தாங்கிச் செல்கிறது
ஒரு வண்ணத்துப் பூச்சி.

In this glee of mutilation
my voice still afloat,
carried across
by a butterfly.

எழுதப்படாமலே போயிருக்க வேண்டிய கவிதை

சவப்பெட்டிகளைத் திறந்து வையுங்கள்

நெடுமரப் பெருநிழல்கள்
ஒடுங்கி,
சோகமாகப்
புற்களின் மேல் விழுந்திருக்கிற
இந்த நிலத்தில்
காற்று எப்போதும் போல
விட்டு விட்டு வீசிக்கொண்டிருக்கிற
நேரத்தில்
இன்னும் நிறைவேறாத ஆசைகளும்
இலட்சியங்களும்
அறுந்து
துயர இழைகளில் ஆடிக்கொண்டிருக்கும்
ஆறடி நீளம் இரண்டடி அகலம்
என ஒரு வெளியில்

அந்த இரு
சவப்பெட்டிகளைத் திறந்து வையுங்கள்
கொஞ்ச நேரமாவது.
புதிய ஆடைகள் வேண்டாம்
அகதி முகாம்களில்
மாற்றுடையின்றித்
தோய்த்த ஆடை
உலரும் வரைக்கும்
மறைப்பினுள் நிற்கும்
நம் பெண்களை நினைப்போம்

குருதி படிந்த அங்கிகளைச்
சற்றே தளர்த்தி
ரணங்களைத் தெரிய விடுவோம்
மெல்லிய வெயில்

A Poem Best Unwritten

Keep the coffins open.

The long shadows of
giant trees
now shrunk
falling sadly
on this soil,
the breeze as always
blowing now and again
where unfulfilled desires
hopes
hang by a thread
on this plot
measuring six by two.

at least for a while
keep those two
coffins open.
No need for
new clothes;
remember,
in those camps
the women
seeking shelter
waiting
for their only clothes
to dry.

Gently open
our blood-stained clothes
reveal our wounds;
let the sun

இலைகளுக்கூடாகப் பூக்களாய்
அவற்றின் மேல் உதிரட்டும்
காற்று வந்து
தடவிச் செல்லட்டும்
தலை சிதறிக்
குருதி நிலம் தெறிக்கக்
கொலை நடந்த இடத்தில்
குருதியில் ஊறிய
சுலோக அட்டை கிடந்ததை
மறுபடியும் அனைவரும் நினைப்போம்.

ஒரு வகையில்,
இந்த உடல்கள் அதிர்ஷ்டம் உள்ளவை
சவப்பெட்டி,
ரப்பர் வாசனையின்றி எரிய
விறகுகள்,
சுற்றி அழச் சுற்றம்,
கண்ணீர் அஞ்சலி,
கவிதை வரியில் துண்டுப்
பிரசுரம்.

பெட்டியில் அடங்கும்
வாய்ப்பே அற்று

மயான மூலையில்
முகமறியா இருளில்
முகமிழந்து புதைந்த உடல்களை,
பாதி எரிந்து
மீதி அழிந்து
சிதைந்த உடல்களைச்
சுதந்திரத்திற்காய்
களத்திலிறங்கிச்
சுதந்திரம் இழந்தவர்களை
நாம் நினையாதிருந்தால்
மிகவும் கொடிது
இது எதிரியின் வேலையல்ல
எம்மவர் கொலைக்கரம்
பதித்த சுவடுகள்

through the leaves,
shine gently on them.
Let the breeze
caress them;
let us remember
again
the heads split open
blood splashing
the placard
now stained
lying on the ground.

Without the comfort
of a coffin.

In a corner of the
cemetery
in pitch black darkness
faceless
buried
half burned
half desecrated bodies;
they fought to be free
and lost their freedom
not to remember them
is callous;
not the work of the enemy
these scars left by
our murderous hands.

Beating the drums
my poetic voice
proclaimed to all:
those are unstained hands.

கறை படியாக் கரங்களெனத்
திக்கெட்டும் பறையறைந்து
கவி சொன்ன
என் வாய்க்குச்
செருப்படி!

நியாயப் படுத்தத் துண்டுப் பிரசுரம்
போலித்தராசு
நீலிக்கண்ணீர்
உதாவது தோழரே,

நமது தேவை:
ஒரு தேசத்தின்
அரசியல் தற்கொலை இதுவென அறியார்
கரங்களில் உயரும்
கருவிகளைப் பறிக்கும்
ஒரு மக்கள் குரல்,

அராஜகத்தின் வேருக்கு
ஒரு கண்ணிவெடி.

Now,
a slap in my face!

Pamphlets to justify
false,
folks,
feigned tears
do not help.

What we need:
the voice of a people
that pluck the weapons
from the raised arms
of those who do not see
the suicide
of a nation.

A bomb to explode
the roots of
oppression.

ஆற்றங்கரையில்

ஆற்றின் இருபுறமும்
காத்திருந்தோம்

காதல் மடிந்துபோன கரைகளில்
இனிமையின் சுவடுகளைச் சொல்ல இருந்த
வெள்ளை மார்புடைய மீன்கொத்தி
பறந்து போயிற்று

ஆற்றைத் தொட்டும் தொடாமலும்
எறிகணையின் வேகத்துடன்
விரைந்து செல்கிறது தலையில்லாக் குருவி
அதன் சிறகுகள்
நீரைத் தொடுகிற போதெல்லாம்
மின் பொறி தெறிக்கிறது

சிறுகுருவி பெரும் ஆற்றுத் தீயை மூட்டுகிறது

படையணியின் முன்னரங்கப் பதுங்கு குழிகளின் மேல்
இன்று
ஒரு போர்க்குரலும் இல்லை

பழகிய வெடி மருந்து மணத்துடன்
பழைய உறவு நீடித்தாலும்
பகைவர் யார்
நண்பர் யார்
என்ற குழப்பத்துடன்
நாளும் இரவும் கவிந்து விலகுகின்ற

பேச்சிழந்தவர்களை
ஆற்றின் மௌனம்

By the River

On both sides of the river
we waited.

On these edges
where love has soured
a white-breasted kingfisher
waiting to sing of good times
now flies away.

A swallow sweeps across
with the speed of a shell
barely touching the water
its feathers
grazing the water
with a shower of sparks.

A small bird creates
a river of fire.

In those trenches
at the edge of the
battleground
no battle cry.

With the familiar smell of
gunpowder
while old friendships linger
who is the enemy
who is the friend
in that confusion
night and day
merge and part.

The silence of the river
carries with it
the voice of those

அடித்துக்கொண்டு செல்கிறது

சிலபோது
எக்காளப் பாடல்கள்
ஆற்றின் மேல்
வெகு உயரத்தில் மோதி மரித்து
இறந்த சொற்களாக விழுகின்றன

மக்காள்,
பிணங்களால் பாலம் அமைத்து
ஆற்றைக் கடக்க வேண்டாம்

நீரைப் பிரிப்பது நிலம்
நிலத்தைப் பிரிப்பது கடல்
காட்டை ஒன்றுமே பிரிப்பதில்லை
பெருமரங்களின் ஆழ ஓடிய வேர்கள் ஊடாக
ஒரு தொடர் கதை
அது
நிலத்தடி ரகசியம்.

who cannot speak.

Sometimes
taunting songs
high above the river
clash and die
fall as lifeless words.

Folks
do not build bridges
with corpses
to cross the river.

The land divides the water,
the sea divides the land,
nothing divides the woods
the roots of the giant trees
run deep
carrying a never-ending tale
a submerged secret.

செம்மணி

சாவும் வாழ்வும் நிறைந்திருந்த பெருந்தெருவில்
திரும்பி வந்தது காற்று

பாலத்தைத் தாண்டியதும்
சற்றே தயங்கியது

பாலத்தின் கீழ் ஒளியில் மினுங்கும் நீர்
நீலமாகவும் பச்சையாகவும் சிவப்பாகவும்
இருந்த நாள்களை இந்தக் காற்று அறியும்

இரக்கமில்லாமல் கடல்நீர் ஏரி மீது
மழை பொழிந்த இரவில்
பீதியும் பெரும் பயமும் விரட்டிய கொடு நடையில்
தாயின் கால் சோர
நீரில் தவறி விழுந்தது குழந்தை

தாத்தாவைத் தாங்கி வந்த கட்டிலே பாடையாக
மழை விட்டும் ஈரக்காற்று ஓயாத சிறு பொழுதில்
தெருவோரமே சுடலையாகிற்று.

எல்லோரும் கடந்து சென்ற பிற்பாடும்
கிராமங்களை நிறைக்கிறது நாயின் ஓலம்

நூறாயிரம் கதைகளைச் சுமந்து
உரம்பெற்றது பாலம்

பாலத்தின் அப்புறம்
சேற்றின் கீழ்ப் புதையுண்டிருந்தவர்களின்
மண்டை ஓடுகளும் எலும்புகளும்
இறகு முளைத்துப் பறந்த பொய்யுரைகள்
வெளியை நிறைக்கின்றன

Crematorium

On this street teeming with life and death
the wind returned.

As it crossed the bridge
it paused.

This wind knew the days
the water glittering in the light
under the bridge
was blue and green and red.

During the days of merciless
rain on this lagoon
panic and fear driving the feet
a mother falters
a child falls into the water.

The bed carrying the elder
becomes a bier
the air still moist
in the morning
the roadside becomes
a crematorium.

After everyone leaves
villages filled with the howl of dogs.

The bridge gathers strength
with the burden of a
thousand stories.

Beyond the bridge
those buried in the mud
their skulls and bones
abruptly disappear
lies fill the air.

என்றாலும்
இப்போது
வெய்யில் பொன் உருக்குகிற மாலை
எல்லாம் தகர்ந்திருந்தாலும்
வெளி அப்படியேயிருக்கிறது
என்கிற தோற்ற மயக்கம்

கைவிலங்குகளுடன் வரும் சமாதானத் தேவதையின்
ஒரு காலடியிலே மறைகிறது வெளி
வெளியில் எழுகின்றது
கடற்கரையை வேலிபோட்டுக்
காவல் இருப்பவனின்
புன்முறுவல் தாங்கிய முகம்

அந்த முகத்தருகே
காற்றையும் நீரையும் காசுக்கு விற்கப்
பெருநிதி சொரிந்து
நிலத்தையும் வளத்தையும் விழுங்குகின்ற
இன்னொரு பிசாசு முகத்தையும் கண்டேன்

பனையளவு உயரத்தில் திடீரென முளைக்கின்றன
முகங்களை விளம்பரப் பலகைகளாக

செம்மணியை மூடியது
செல்ஃபோன்

நூறாயிரம் கதைகளைச் சுமந்து
உரம்பெற்ற பாலத்தை
இப்போது
உடைத்து விடுகிறது ஒரு கண்ணீர்த் துளி.

Even so
now
an evening bathed in golden light
all things have changed
except the illusion
of an unchanging land.

The land now covered
by angels of peace
carrying shackles.
On this land
the sea fenced off, and
the smiling face
of the guard.

Beside that face
yet another
equally devilish
flinging money
for the right to sell
air and water
gobbling the land
gobbling its wealth.

Faces become billboards
to the height of palmyrah trees.

The crematorium
now eclipsed
by cell phones.

A bridge nourished
by a thousand stories
now
broken by a tear drop.

துண்டிக்கப்பட்ட காலின் கதை

துண்டிக்கப்பட்ட காலின் கதையை எழுதுகிறேன்

மலைகளிலிருந்து இறங்கிப்
பாலை வெளியூடாக நகரம் நோக்கிச்
செல்கிற தெரு ஒன்று
இப்போது குற்றுயிராகக் கிடக்கிறது

போரின் வரலாறு குருதியில் குழைத்துத்
தூவி விட்டிருக்கிற சித்திரங்கள்
தெருவின் மீது துயர் தீராத
ஆவியாய்த் தொடர்கின்றன

காயம் பட்ட மரங்களின் கண்ணீர்
உதவி தர வந்த வெளிநாட்டாரின்
வாகனங்கள் விட்டுச் செல்கிற
தடங்களின் மீது படிகிறது

உரிமை கோரப்படாத உடலை
அசிரத்தையுடன் மூடும்
பிண அறைப்பணியாளனைப் போல

புழுதி கண்ணீரை மூடுகிறது

படை எடுப்புகளால் துவண்டாலும்
தெரு இருக்கிறது.

கண்டேன்.
தெரு
வழி பிரியும் சந்தியொன்றில்
பாதி உடைந்திருந்த வழி காட்டிக் கல் ஒன்றை
அதன் மீது
குந்தி இருந்தது ஒரு மண்டை ஓடு.

The Story of a Severed Leg

I am writing the story of a severed leg.

A road that begins in the mountains
runs through this barren land
to the city,
now lies distraught.

The story of war mixed with blood
in scattered fragments
like restless ghosts,
follow the road in grief.

The tears of wounded trees,
settle on the marks
left by vehicles
of well-meaning NGOs.

The dust covers the tears,

indifferent, like an undertaker
covering the body
of an unclaimed corpse.

Dismembered by war,
the road survives;
I saw;
where the road forks,
a half-broken milestone;

on it sat
a skull.

நீரற்ற நெடுந் தெருவில்
தாகம் பெருக்கெடுக்கக்
காட்டின் உயிர் நாடியை நோக்கித்
திரும்பிய போது
கண்டேன்:
பாலை மரத்தின் கீழ்த்
துண்டிக்கப்பட்ட கால் ஒன்றை.

எவ்வித முறைப்பாடுகளுமற்றுக் கிடந்த
அந்தக் காலிலிருந்து
ஆயிரம் கதைகள் எழுந்து
காடுகளை நிறைத்தன.

நினைவறியாப் பொழுதொன்றில் காடுகள்
உருவான போது
அவற்றுடன் கூடப் பிறந்த
மாயத் தோற்றங்களையும் ஐதீகங்களையும்
இந்தக் கதைகள்
இப்போது இடம் பெயர்த்து விட்டன.

இடம்பெயர்ந்த மாயக்கதைகளும் ஐதீகங்களுமோ
புலம் பெயர்ந்த நாடுகளில்
தமிழர் கோவில்களிலும் வாழ்க்கைக் கோலங்களிலும்
பாவச் சின்னங்களாகத்
தொங்கிக் கொண்டிருக்கின்றன

அவற்றின் கீழ்
இருட்டறைகளில் கழிவிரக்கமும்
தொலைவு தரும் பொறுப்பின்மையும் படர
உலவி வரும் நடைப் பிணங்களைக்
கண்டேன்.

கண்டேன்
வலி, வீரம், துன்பம், கொடுமை,
ஆற்றாமை - எல்லாவற்றினதும்
தாங்கு நிலமாக இருந்த காட்டில்
துண்டிக்கப்பட்ட கால் ஒன்றை.

On this barren road
consumed with thirst
turning toward the forest,
I saw,
beneath the Palai tree
a severed leg.

A thousand stories
rose to fill the forest
from that leg
lying without protest.

Those stories displaced
the wondrous tales and visions
the forest acquired at birth,
long before memory's time.

The displaced stories and beliefs
in diasporic lands
in the temples of Tamils,
in their myriad lives,
now hang,
embodiments of sin.

Beneath those,
compassion in darkened rooms,
the irresponsibility of distance,
I see
in these walking corpses.

I saw
in the forest engulfing
pain, courage, sorrow, oppression,
despair – the severed leg.

கண்டேன்
எனது கனவின் கல்லறைகள் மீது
தனது கதைகளை
மௌனமாக எறிந்து கொண்டேயிருக்கும்
துண்டிக்கப்பட்ட கால் ஒன்றை.

I saw,
on the tomb of my dreams,
scattering its stories
in silence,
the severed leg.

புதைகுழிப் பாடல்

அவன் தனியே
அவர்களோ மூவர்
முகம் தெரியா இருள்
அவர்களுடைய மனதைப் போல

தன்னுடைய புதைகுழியைத்
தானே வெட்டும் அவலம்
நேர்ந்தபோது
அவன் என்ன உணர்ந்திருப்பான்
என்பது
வார்த்தைக்குள் அகப்படாத
குரூரம்.

அந்தப் புதைகுழியின் மேல்
காற்றில்
உறைந்து போயிருக்கின்றன
அவன் இறுதியாகச்
சொன்ன வார்த்தைகள்

காற்று அவற்றைக்
கொண்டு செல்லாது

மழையும் சூரியனும்
கிட்டவும் நெருங்கா

அவன் சொல்லாத வார்த்தைகளோ
மண்ணுட் போய்
மண்ணிலிருந்து மரத்துட் போய்
அங்கிருந்து கிளைக்கு
கிளையில் இருந்து இலைக்கு
இலையிலிருந்து காற்றில்
இடையறாமல்
அலையலையாக எழுந்து கொண்டிருக்கிறது.

GRAVESONG

He by himself,
three of them,
impenetrable darkness,
like their hearts.

The torment
of digging
his own grave;
he then understood
a violence
beyond words.

On that grave
in the air,
frozen
his final words.

The wind will not
scatter it,
the rain and sun,
will not dare approach it.

His unsaid words
entered the earth
passed from earth to tree,
then to branches,
finally to leaves,
and now in the wind
they rise in waves
unceasingly.

அந்தப் புதைகுழியின் மேல்
பிசாசு இல்லை
தெய்வமும் இல்லை
நினைவுச் சின்னம் எனவும் ஒன்றில்லை

ஆளரவமற்ற இரவுத் தெருவின்
ஒற்றை விளக்குப் போல
உதிரியாய் ஒரு பட்டிப் பூ
அதன்மீது
காலம் தன்னுடைய கொடூர
நகங்களைப் பதித்துள்ளது.

அவனுடைய இறுதி வார்த்தைகளில்
இருந்தது
நமது தேசத்தின் உயிர்.

On that grave
there is no ghost,
no god either,
this is no memorial stone.

Like a solitary lamp
in an empty street,
one stray flower;
on that
time has left
its cruel fingers.

In his final words
lay
the life of our land.

மயான காண்டம்

அன்றைய இரவு
அடர்ந்ததான கறுப்புப் போர்வையுள்
பூமி இருந்ததாய் எனக்குத் தெரிந்தது
அதுவுமல்லாமல்
வெளிச்சம் இருந்த ஞாபகமும் இன்றி
ஓலையின் அசைவு, ஒரு குழந்தையின் அழுகை
தொலைவிருந்து எழுந்து வருகிற ரயிலின் நீண்ட குரல்
ஒன்றுமில்லாது ஒரு எழுதப்படாத சோகம்

பாருங்கள்
ஒரு கதை போல சனங்கள்
எனக்கு அதைச் சொல்ல முன்பு
அன்றைய இரவு நான் உணர்ந்த சோகம்
அதிசயமில்லையா?

முகமும் விழிகளும் இல்லாத வெறும் மனிதர்களுக்கு
அவனது மரணம் ஒரு செய்தி போல
நீளவும் தூக்கம் வரும்வரை
கதைக்கிற செய்தி

இன்றைக்கு இரவு அன்று போலல்ல
நிலவு தெறித்த இலைகள் சுவரில் மிதக்கின்றன
விளக்கில்லாத தெருவில் விட்டில்களும் இல்லை
நான் இதை எழுதத் தொடங்கும் போது
முகமற்றவர்கள் தூங்கப் போய்விட்டார்கள்

அன்றிரா
நான் போனபோது
வைத்தியசாலையில், "கேற்" றின் வெளிப்புறம்

Closure

That night,
a deep blanket of darkness
shrouded the land;
also,
without the memory of light,
the palms swayed,
a child cried,
the wail of a distant train,
nothing, an unwritten grief.

Listen,
before the people
told me this
just another story,
that night I felt this grief;
surprising, isn't it?

For people without faces or eyes
his death
was just another occurrence,
something to talk about
until they fall asleep.

Tonight is unlike then,
the moon-splattered leaves
float on the walls,
no flying insects
in the lampless streets;
when I began to write,
the faceless ones had
gone to sleep.

That night,
when I went
to the hospital

குனிந்த தலையுடன் நின்றனர் சிலர்
மிக மெதுவாக உள்ளே சென்று
வைத்தியசாலையின் நீள நடந்து
மாடிப்படிகளை நுனிக்கால் கடக்க

18ஆம் வார்ட்
விறாந்தையில் கூட ஓரிரு கட்டில்கள்
விளக்கு வெளிச்சம், வெள்ளைச் சீருடை
அங்கேதான் உன்னை வளர்த்தியிருந்தனர்

வெண்முகில் பரப்பாய் உயர இருந்து
கட்டிலின் விளிம்பு வரையும் தொங்கிய
வெண்ணிறத் துகிலை நீக்கி
உடலைக் காட்டினாள் ஒருத்தி
மற்றவள்
ஒருபுறம் சரிந்து கிடந்த முகத்தை
ஓரக்கைகளால் அசைத்து நிமிர்த்தவும்
ஒருகணம்
எனது குருதி நாடிகள் உறைந்து போயின
கால்களின் கீழே
பூமி பிளந்து சரிவதான உணர்வு எழுந்தது

என்ன விதமாய் இப்படி நிகழ்ந்தது?

உன் நிமிர்ந்த நடையும் நறுக்கிய மீசையும்
சுருண்டு கிடந்த குழல்களும்
எனது நினைவில் இருந்தன
வடலிகள் விரியும் சுடலையின் பக்கமும்
கிழக்கே பனைவெளிப் புறத்திலும்
அப்பால் உயனை வெளியிலும்
உனது ஆடுகள் திரிய
அவற்றின் பின்
நீ சீட்டி ஒலியுடன் தொடர்தலும்

outside the gate, a few stood
their heads bowed.

I walked gingerly inside
across the hospital,
tiptoed up the stairs,

ward number 18;
a few beds even on the verandah
lamp light, white uniforms,
you were laid out.

A white cloud from top
to the edge of the bed,
she lifted the sheet
showed me your body,
another tilted your face
with the edge of her palm;
in that one instant,
my heart froze;
beneath my feet
the world split and sank.

How did this occur?

Your upright walk, twirled
moustache, wavy locks,
I remember;
where the fences lead,
towards the cemetery,
in the east among palmyrah trees,
your goats stray,
and you follow, whistling,
I remember.

எனது நெஞ்சில் உள்ளது
செம்மண் நிலத்தின் மார்பு பிளந்து
வேர்விடும் கிளுவையை, சிவப்பு முள்முருக்கை
தோண்டவே உயரும் அலவாங்கின் நுனி
எவ்விதம் உனது நெஞ்சுள் இறங்கிற்று?

முன்னைய நாளின் நினைவுகள்
எனது நெஞ்சில் இருந்தன

பொன்வண்டுகள் மினுங்கும் என்று
இலந்தை மரங்களை மேய்ந்து திரிந்ததும்
மணிப்புறா பிடிக்க வைத்த கண்ணியில்
அடுத்த வீட்டுக் கோழிகள் நெரிந்ததும்
உனக்கும் தெரியும்
மீண்டும் மீண்டும் பிள்ளையார் கோயிலின்
தீர்த்தக் கரையில் குந்தி இருந்ததும்
பயறு கொய்ததும்
பாய் விரித்தது பசும்புல் என்று
படுத்துக் கிடந்ததும்
அடுத்த வீட்டுச் சந்திரன் "அலி" எனச் சொன்னதில்
அவனை இழுத்து வந்து அப்பால் விரிந்த
சணல் மரப்புதர்களுள் அவனைப் புரட்டி
இடுப்பில் இருந்த துணியை உருவித்
திகைப்புக் கொண்டதும் திரும்பிப் பறந்ததும்

இவற்றை மறத்தல் இயலுமா எனக்கு?
மேற்கே போனாய் நீ
நான் இன்னும் கிழக்கே நடந்தேன்
நண்ப,
இன்று இப்படித்தான் உனைக் காண நேர்கிறது
இரத்தமும் சதையும்
நிணமும் எலும்பும்

Trees
splitting asunder
the chest of the red earth
grow their roots;
the tip of the spike
that uproots them,
how did it enter
your chest?

Those early days
were still in my heart.

Scouring Ilanthai trees,
convinced that golden beetles
would glitter;
the traps for pigeons,
snare the neighbour's fowls,
all thesc you kncw;
seated on the ghats
of the Pillayar temple
time and again,
munching nuts,

lying on grass,
a carpet rolled out for you,
suspecting next-door Chandran
to be a eunuch
dragging him to the bushes,
pulling off his cloth
rushing back
amazed,
how could I forget these?
You went west,
I traveled east,
my friend, today

அன்று
வானை நோக்கி எலும்புகள் நீட்டி
செத்துப்போன ராட்சத மரமாய்
நெருப்பில் கருகி நின்றது வீடு
உனது வீட்டை இரவில் கொளுத்தினர்

சூரியன் பிளந்து சிதறும் குருதியாய்
கிடுகுகள் விலக்கி ஒளிரும் கதிர்களை
தெருவில் நின்று பார்க்க நேர்ந்தது
உனது நிலத்தை அவர்கள் பறித்தனர்

இன்று
உன்னைக் கொன்றனர்
உன்னை அவர்கள் கொன்றனர்

இன்றோ
பழைய கதையை மீண்டும் பார்க்கிறேன்
ஆவரசஞ் செடி, அதன்புறம் கள்ளி
ஆட்களே இன்றிச் சூரியன் மட்டும் தனித்துப் போன
இவ்வெளியில்
இன்றும்
ஆள்காட்டிகளே கூக்குரல் எழுப்ப
உன்னை எரித்துத் திரும்பினர்
பிறகு நாங்களும்

நெருஞ்சி மலர்கள் மஞ்சளாய் நிமிர்கிற மண்ணில்
ஒருபிடி கூட உனக்குச் சொந்தமில்லை
உனது அப்பன்
பனையில் இருந்து தவறி விழுந்ததில்
ஒரு கணப்பொழுதில் வார்த்தைகள் இழந்து
ரத்தமாய் உறைந்தவன்
அவனது அப்பன்
செத்துப்போனதும்

I have to see you like this,
blood, flesh,
guts and bones.

That day,
stretching its bones to the sky
a dead giant tree,
your house stood gutted;

your house they burned in the night.

The sun split
into streams of blood;
the flames shooting between
the roof;
we watched from the roof.

They took your land,
today,
you were killed;
they killed you.
Today,
I relive that tale,
the sun alone
no people on these plains,
the lapwing's cry of death,
they returned
after burning you,
later we too
came back.

In this land,
where Nerunji blooms yellow
you don't own
a handful of earth;

“காய்க்கும் நன்றாய்” என்பதனாலே
மாதுளம் பாத்தியுள் ஆழப்புதைந்தவன்
இன்று
ஒன்றுமேயில்லை
உன்னையும் வெட்டினர்
ஆயிரம் விரல்கள் உன்னை நோக்கி
துவக்கு முனைகளாய் நீண்டபோதும்
கோடையில் வெடிக்கிற யாழ்ப்பாணத்தின்
பாலைமண்ணில் உறுதியாய் நிமிர்ந்தாய்

உன்னைக் கொன்றனர்
உன்னை அவர்கள் கொன்றனர்
எழுதப்படாத சரித்திரம்
துயர் சூழ்ந்து
ரத்தம் சிந்திய நிலங்களின் மீது
நெல் விளைகிறது;சணல் பூக்கிறது
மழை பெய்கிறது

நீ துயில்க
அந்நியர்கள் வந்துவிட்டார்கள் என்பதையாவது
நான்
அவர்களுக்கு நினைவூட்ட வேண்டும்.

your father,
from the palmyrah
slipped and fell,
in a moment,
he lost his voice and froze;
his father
when he died was
buried deep
so fruits could thrive;
today, there is nothing,
they cut you up;
when a thousand fingers
tips of rifles
stretched towards you
in the barren Jaffna land
you walked upright.

You were killed;
they killed you.

An unwritten tale;
on this land,
struck by grief,
streaming blood,
paddy grows; chanal flowers bloom,
rain pours.

Sleep well,
outsiders have arrived;
of that,
I must remind them.

நடுவெளி

பெருவெளியில்
இரு பனைமரங்கள்
சூரியனை உயர்த்திப் பிடித்தபடி நின்றன
அவற்றிடையே விழுந்து கிடந்த
ஒற்றையடிப் பாதை
நடுவழியில் முறிந்து விட்டது

இப்புறம்
தெரு இருந்த சுவடே தெரியவில்லை

வீடு அழிந்த திசைநோக்கியே
எப்போதும் அசையும்
வெப்பக் காற்றில்
இறந்துபோன கடலின் நெடி

வாழ்விழந்த நாள் விலகும்
பாழ்நிலத்தில் புல் விரியும்
என
தீயில் மிதந்து
திரும்பி நடந்து வந்தால்

கால் பதிக்க முடியாமல்
எப்புறமும் கண்ணிவெடி

இவ்வழியா
அவ்வழியா
எவ்வழியில் இருந்தது மலைவேம்பு?

சுமைதாங்கி
அதனோரம்
நீர்த்தொட்டி

Wilderness

In that wide expanse,
two palmyrah trees
hold up the sun;
fallen between them
a narrow pathway
now sundered.

From here,
not even traces remain.

In the hot wind
always blowing towards
the destroyed house,
the wail of a dead sea.

The desolate days will end,
the wasteland will thrive,
we hope,
floating on fire, then
walking back home;

landmines everywhere,
no place to step,

was it here,
or there,
that margosa tree?

A shelter,
by its side,
a water trough,
a little further

சிறு தொலைவில் ஆவுரஞ்சிக் கல்
எல்லாம் இருந்த வழியெங்கே?

யாரெடுத்துச் சொல்வார்?

ஓங்கிக் குரல்கொடுக்க

பூமிக்கும் இல்லை பொறுமை

எனச் சொல்லி சிரிப்போர்
குரல் கேட்டேன்.

a rubbing stone
for cattle;

who will speak for these?

to shout aloud,

        even the earth disdains,

say some in derision,
I hear their voice.

கல்வெட்டு

கூடு திரும்பின பறவைகள்

அந்தியின் கடைசி வெளிச்சத் துளி
தெருமுனையில்,
தொலைதூரம் விழிநீளம் காத்திருக்கும்
அம்மாவின் முகத்தில்
இருள் ஏற்றுகிறது

மூடப்பட்ட பாடசாலைக் கதவுகளில்
வெறுமை
வகுப்பறைகளில் நிராசையின்
கோலம்

அவன் வீடு திரும்பவில்லை
நாடு கலங்கிற்று ஒரு நாள்

இரும்பின் தடங்களும், ஈயக்குண்டுகளும்
எரியும் நெருப்பும் சூழ அவன்
எதிரியின் தளத்தை நொருக்கிய போது
காற்றில் கோவில் மணி அலறிற்று
வீட்டில்
கண்ணீர் அலையென ஓடிற்று

அவன் சொன்ன வார்த்தைகளுமில்லை
எங்களுக்குச் சொல்ல வார்த்தைகளும் இல்லை.

Obituary

The birds flew home.

At the end of the street
a glimmer of ebbing light,
gazing into the distance, waiting,
Amma's face,
gradually clouds over.

School doors remain shut,
empty,
in the classrooms,
despair.

He did not return home;
on that day, the land shook.

Mangled steel, flying bullets,
engulfed by flames
when he smashed the enemy's hold,
the temple bells wailed;
at home
tears welled and flowed.

He said nothing
We had nothing to say.

இறுதி வார்த்தை

இன்று
மயிரிழையில் ஆடிக்கொண்டிருக்கிறது
வாழ்வு.

குருதி கொப்புளித்துப்
பிரவாகம் எடுக்கும் கண்களுடன்
மரணத்தின் படைவீரர்கள்
எந்த நேரமும் வரலாம்.

குருட்டு விசுவாசமுள்ள
முரட்டுப் போர்க்குணத்துக்கும்
முரட்டு விசுவாசமுள்ள
குருட்டுப் போர்க்குணத்துக்கும்
நன்றி.

மனிதம் உருவழிகையில்
மௌனத் திரையிறக்கி
நிஷ்டை கூடுதல்
கவிஞனுக்கு அப்பாற்பட்டது.
பேசுகிற கவிஞன் ஒரு கண்ணிவெடி
பேசாதவன் பிறகு
பிரளயமாவான்.

வாழ்வு,
காற்றொரு துளியும்
கடலொரு பிடியும்
புணர்ந்து பிறந்த நுரை அல்ல
என்பதை

எல்லோரும் உணர வேண்டும்.
மேலும்
இரத்தம் எப்போதும் சிவப்பு அல்ல

Last Words

Today
life
hangs by a thread.

Blood boiling
eyes ablaze
the soldiers of death
may appear
at any time.

Blind devotion
to a violent aggression
a violent devotion
to a blind aggression
I thank you.

When people die
to shroud in silence
withdraw into silence
is not for the poet.
A poet who speaks
a land mine
who does not
the voice of doom.

A drop of air
a handful of water
the foam they create
do not make life.

This you must
understand;
you must know

உறைந்த பிறகு
கறுப்பு என்பதையும்.

நல்லவை, அல்லவை
எல்லாவற்றையும் தீயிலிடும்
ஒரு கண்மூடித்தனமான கேள்விக்கு
வேத மந்திர கோஷம் முழங்க,
எல்லா இடங்களிலிருந்தும்
வருகிறது காளான்.

நட்பும்
நேசமும்
நியாயமும்
நுழைய முடியாமல்
உறைந்த பருத்தி ஆடைகளுக்குள்ளும்
தடித்த முதலைத் தோலுக்குள்ளும்
இருண்டு கிடக்கின்ற
இதயத்தின் அறைகளுக்குள்
எங்காவது ஒரு மூலைக்கு

எரியும் என் சிதை
ஒரு சிறு வெளிச்சம் தரட்டும்.

அந்த வெளிச்சத்திலிருந்து
ஒரு பாடல் பிறக்கும்.

வீரம் விளைந்த சிந்தப்படாத
இரத்தத்தின் கறை படிந்த
கரங்களால்
குழந்தைகளை, கவிதைகளை
மலர்களைத் தொடாமல்...

that blood is not
always red, congeals
into black.

A blind faith
that throws all
good and evil
into the fire;
from everywhere
singing praises
mushrooming hordes.

Friendship
love
truth
cannot pierce
the coarse cotton clothes
the thick alligator skins;
in the dark
room of the heart
somewhere in a corner

let my pyre burn
to shed a tiny light.

From that light
a song will appear.

With those battle hardened
blood-stained hands,
do not touch
children, poems
flowers . . .

நான் இறந்து போகிறபோது

நான் இறந்து போகிறபோது
என்ன நடக்கும்?

அது ஒரு காலைப் பொழுதானால்
நிலவு எழும்

மாலையானால்
தேர்க்கால்கள் ஒடிந்து விழக்
காத்திருக்கும் சூரியனின்
கண்ணசைவில் காலத்தின் நிறம் பிரியும்

இரவெனில்
பறவைகள் தூக்கம் தொலைத்து விழித்தெழுந்து
பாடும்

அந்தப் பாடலின் அலைகளில்
சாக்குருவியின் இறகுகள் தீப்பட்டெரியும்.

நான் இறந்து போகிறபோது
என்ன நடக்கும்?

காற்றில்லாத போதும்
எல்லாக் கதவுகளும் சாளரங்களும்
தாமாகத் திறந்துகொள்ளும்
சங்கீதமும் அழுகையும்
ஒன்றை வெட்டி ஒன்றென மாறி மாறி எழும்

நான் இறந்து போகிறபோது
நிசப்தத்தின் உள்ளொலியில் கவிதை எழுகிறது

When I Die and Depart

What will happen
when I die and depart?

If it happens to be dawn
the moon will rise.

If it happens to be evening,
as the wheels of the chariot crumble,
in the wink of the waiting sun
the light will blaze.

If it happens to be night
the birds, woken from sleep,
will sing.

In the melody of that song
The feathers of the lapwing will burn.

What will happen
when I die and depart?

Without the wind
the doors and windows
will fly open;
Song and dirge
will meld together

When I die and depart
a poem will rise from the sound of silence.

When I am dead
do not close the front door

நான் இறந்த பிற்பாடோ
தலைவாசலை மூடாதே
கிடுகு வேலி பிரித்த மாற்று வழியும் தேவையில்லை
நான் போக
வெறும் நீரைச் சிந்தவிடு
என்னுடலில்
நான் எரிவேன்

நான் இறந்த பிற்பாடு

புற்களின் கண்ணீர்த்துளி
இருளின் குருதி
பூமியின் நரம்புகளில் துயர் மீட்ட வரும்
கடலோரக் காற்று

வெளியில் ஆடும் விளக்கு.

do not tear the fence
for another pathway.
As I leave
spill water
on my body,
I will burn

After I am dead

the tears of the grass
the blood of the night
the breeze from the sea
to strum the grief of the land

the swaying lamp.

Love

இறந்த காலம்

யாருமற்ற தெருவில்
மழையில்,
ஒரு வாகை மரத்தடியில்
திடீரென

உன்னைக் காண்பேன் என
நம்புதல் இயலாது,
ஆயினும் நடந்தது.

நெடுநாளின் பின்
வண்ணத்துப் பூச்சியாய்த்
துடிக்கிற உனது இமைகளை,
புத்தகக் கட்டையும், குடையையும்
இறுகப் பற்றியிருந்தும்
நடுங்கும் விரல்களைப் பார்க்கிறேன்.

முகம்,
திருப்பவும் முடியாது
மழை,
விட்டு
விலகவும் இயலாது
மழை.

'வெயில் வா, மழை போ'
என்று மனதில்
செபிக்கிறாய் போல

என் சின்னப் பெண்ணே

எமது,
அன்றைய சூரியன்
அன்றே மறைந்து
போயிற்று.

The Past

A deserted street,
in the rain,
in the canopy of a tree,
suddenly

to see you
seemed unlikely but
it did happen.

After so long,
your eyes fluttering,
coloured butterflies
grasping an umbrella,
and a bundle of books.
I see the trembling fingers,
you were stunned.

Face,
you cannot turn away,
rain;
leaving,
not possible,
rain.

Rain, go away;
Sun, come again,
you seem to chant to yourself,

my little girl,

the Sun
of our past
on that day,
disappeared.

ஒரு சிங்களத் தோழிக்கு எழுதியது

நெல் விதைப்பதற்குப் பதிலாகத்
துப்பாக்கி ரவைகளையே விதைக்கும்
எங்கோ ஒரு கண்காணாத தொலைவில்,
பாதி மாடிவீடுகளாகவும்
பாதி ‘பயங்கரவாதி’ களாகவும்
நிறைந்திருப்பதாகச் சொல்லக் கேட்ட
ஓர் இடத்தில் இருந்து வந்த
சாதாரண மனிதனான என்னைச்
சந்தித்த அதிர்ச்சியிலிருந்து
நீங்களும்
உங்கள் நண்பர் குழுவும்
விடுபட
நீண்டநாளாகாது.

மண் கலங்க ஓர் நிறமும்,
மண்ணோடு நீர் கலங்க
நீரில் நிழல் விரிக்கும் மேகங்களால்
ஓர் நிறமும்,
மின்னுவதற்கென்றே
நிலவின் திரை நூலிழையில்
போர்வையிட்ட
பாலாவி நீர்ப்பரப்பின்
படித்துறையில்,
அருகமர்ந்து
இனிய குரலில்
உங்கள் சிங்களப் பாடலைக்
கேட்கிறபோது
நான் மனம் கிளர்ந்தேன்.

முன்னர் ஒருதரம்,
அப்போது நான் சிறுவன்,

To a Sinhalese Girl

You have heard
we come from far way,
beyond the horizon
where bullets are sown
in fields,
not grain,
where plush houses abound
and terrorists breed;
your surprise
at meeting me
an ordinary man,
will soon fade from you
and your friends.

On the banks of Palaavi
now the colour of muddied sand;
yet another
as the clouds
spread a blanket of shade
on the muddied water;
the canopy of the moon
finely embroidered
to make the water glitter;
seated on the ghat,
I listen
to the melody
of your Sinhala songs
and my heart melts.

Once in the past,
a boy then,

மாகோ ரயில் நிலையத்தில்
மட்டக்களப்பு ரயிலுக்காகக்
காத்திருக்கையில்,
அப்பாவோடு
தண்டவாளத்தில் கொஞ்சநேரம்
நீள நடந்தபோது.
நடு இரவு,

மெல்லிய குரலில்
ஓர் தாலாட்டுப் பாடல்
காற்றில் அனுங்கிற்று,
குழந்தையின் அழுகுரல் இடை
அம் மெல்லிய குரலின் அதிர்வு
அவ்விரவு,
எனது மனதை நெகிழ்த்திற்று
நான் துயருற்றேன்.

இன்றும்,
மெல்லிய துயர்
எனைச் சூழ்ந்தது.

ஆடியிலே தூங்கும்வரை
ஓயாத பெருங்காற்று,
ஓயாத பெருங்காற்றில்
உதிர்கின்ற பொன்னொச்சிப்
பூக்களையும்,
நெடுந்தோகை மயில்
தனது நடையின் திசைமாற்றத்
தடுமாறும் கணங்களையும்
புன்சிரிப்போடு
பார்த்து ரசிக்கப்
புரியாத மொழி நம்மைத்
தொலைவிலா வைத்தது?

at the Maho station
while waiting with my father
for the train,
walking along the tracks
at midnight
in low tones
a lullaby wafted
across.
The child's sniffles
and the lilting song
that night
pierced my heart;
I was saddened.

A gentle grief
surrounds me
today.

Till end of July
a gusty wind;
in the blowing wind
the ponnochi flowers
shed their petals;
the long-feathered peacock
flustered
as its step falters;
from relishing these sights
with a smile,
do our languages
separate us?

To please you,
I cannot even
pluck a feather from

உங்களுக்கு விருப்பம்
என்பதற்காக
என்னால் ஒரு மயிலிறகாவது
பறித்துத் தர முடியவில்லை
முன்னிரவில்
புல் வழியில்
முழு நிலவில் நடந்துபோக
நீங்கள் விரும்பிய போதும்
என்னால் துணைவர முடிந்ததில்லை.

மெல்லிய ஏமாற்றங்களை மறக்க
உங்கள் கண்களுக்கு முடியவில்லை.
உங்கள் மெல்லிய நேசத்தை மறக்க
எனக்கும் முடியவில்லை.

இயற்கையின் கழுத்தை நெரிக்காமல்
பூக்களை மலரவிட்டுப்
புற்களைப் பூக்கவிட்டுப்
போய்விட்டோம்.

நீங்கள் தெற்காக
நானோ வடக்காக
மலைத் தொடரின் மாபெரிய
மரங்களுக்கு மேலாகக்
குளிர்காற்று இறங்கிவரும்
இளங்காலைப் பொழுதில்
பல் துலக்கும்போது
பயிலும் சிறுநடையில்,
மாந்தையில்
மூடுண்ட நகரை மீட்க முயலும்
ஆய்வு வேலையில்
கொஞ்சநாள் இணைந்ததை
நீங்கள் நினைப்பீர்கள்.
உங்களுடைய மக்களுக்குச்

the peacock for you;
in the early evening
on the grassy plain
under a full moon
in spite of your wish
I couldn't accompany you.

Your eyes will not forget
these mild disappointments;
and I could not forget
your gentle love.

Without strangling nature
we let the flowers bloom
the grass grow,
we left.

You to the south
me going north
in the dawn
when from the mountains
from above the trees
a gentle breeze
descends;
when brushing your teeth
while meandering
in the midst of your work
seeking to reclaim
the city
you will remember
our brief encounter.

Tell your people,
here too

சொல்லுங்கள் :
இங்கும் பூக்கள் மலர்கின்றன.
புற்கள் வாழ்கின்றன.
பறவைகள் பறக்கின்றன.

the flowers bloom
the grass grows
and birds fly.

சமாந்தரம் கொள்ளாத உலகங்கள்

இரண்டு பெண்கள்,
இரண்டு ஆடுகள்.

அறுவடை முடித்த வயல்வெளி
கடந்து,
கிழக்கே நடந்தனர்.
கிழக்கிலும் வயல்வெளி
நீளம் நீளமாய் வரம்பு தெரிந்தது.
நீலம் நீலமாய் வானம் விரிந்தது.

மஞ்சள் மலர்கள் பூத்து நிறைந்தன,
சணல் மரப் புதர்களுள்
மைனாக் குருவிகள்,
மெல்ல எழுந்து வெளியே பறந்தன.

இரண்டு பெண்கள்
ஒருத்தி சிறியவள்
மற்றவள் உடலை இளமை மெதுவாய்ப்
போர்த்தி இருந்தது
முன்னும் பின்னுமாய்
இரண்டு ஆடுகள் நடந்து சென்றன

இடையில் நின்று
அறுகம் புற்களில் முதுகைத் தேய்த்து
மீண்டும் நடந்தன

அடிவான் சரிவில் நீண்டதான
சமாந்தர ரேகைகள் விழுத்தியபடி
ஒரு விமானம் எழுந்தது.
எழவும்,
வயல்வெளி இருந்த விழிகள் நான்கும்

Not Parallel Worlds

Two girls,
two goats.

They cross
a harvested field,
walk eastward;
more fields in the east,
stretches and stretches of bunds
blue expanding to blue skies.

Yellow flowers in bloom;
from chanal bushes
mynah birds
emerge to gently fly away.

Two girls,
one younger,
the other gently smothered
in youth;
front and rear,
walked two goats.

They pause,
rub their backs in the grass
and continue.

In the horizon, shedding
long parallel lines
a plane arose;
seeing it rise,
the four eyes in the field
scan the expanse of sky;

விண்வெளிப் பரப்பில்
சில கணம் தரிக்க
அமைதி தழுவி இருந்த வெளிகளில்
மெல்லிய அதிர்வு

இன்னும் விரைவாய் விமானம் உயரும்
இன்னும் சமாந்தர ரேகைள் வரையும்
மாலைக் காற்றுக் கூந்தலை வருட
வரம்பு நீளத் தம் வழி தொடரும்

இரண்டு பெண்கள்
இரண்டு ஆடுகள்.

in the quiet plains
a gentle shudder.

The plane climbs higher
the parallel lines stretch further;
the evening breeze ruffles their hair
along the bunds they journey on.

Two girls,
two goats.

சடங்கு

பிறகு
அனைவரும் அமர்ந்தனர்

நாற்சார் வீடு
நடுவில் நீளமாய்,
மேசை போட்டுத், துணிவிரித்துக்
காணி எழுதி வீடு எழுதிப்
படம் எடுத்து,
காசெண்ணிப் பார்த்துத்
தலையாட்டி
அதையும் படமெடுத்து
பெரிய புத்தகங்களில்
குனிந்தபடி கையெழுத்து வைத்து
மோதிரமும் மாற்றிய

பிறகு,
அனைவரும் அமர்ந்தனர்,
நிலத்தில்.

இரவுதானே!
இட்டலி சாப்பாடென்று ஆக
குழந்தைகளும் அலறித்
தூங்க ஆரம்பித்த

பிறகு,
மறுபடியும் அவளருகே அமர்ந்தான்
கொஞ்சம் சிநேகத்துடன்
'அவன்'.

Ritual

Later,
they all sat down.

In the centre
of a courtyard house
a long table,
covered with cloth;
the land transferred,
the house given away,
pictures taken,
money counted
heads nodding,
that too photographed;
in large ledgers,
they stoop to sign;
next the exchange of rings.

Then
all sat down
on the floor.

Evening isn't it?
A meal of idli,
bawling kids
settling to sleep,

then
he sat by her side again,
more friendly now;
"He."

கோடை வயல்

வரம்புகள் நீளம் போகும்
வயல்களை ஊடறுத்து

சணல் மரம் வரம்பு மேவ
வயல்களோ மஞ்சள் பூக்கள்
கோவிலின் குளத்து மேட்டில்
ஆடு போய்ப் புல்லு மேயும்
அகட்டிய கிளைகளோடு மருது
அதன் கிளைகளுள் ஒன்றில் ஏணை

குழந்தையின் அழுகை கேட்கும்

நடுகையை நடுவில் விட்டுக்
குழந்தைக்கு முலை திறந்தாள்

வெற்றிலை போட்ட வாயில்
குருதியின் சிவப்பு மின்ன

வயலுக்கு மீண்டாள், மீண்டும்
குழந்தையின் அழுகை கேட்கும்.

Summer Fields

The long bunds
criss-cross the fields.

The chanal tree spreads
above the bund,
yellow flowers cover the fields;
on the ghats of the temple pond
the sheep graze,
the spreading branches of the tree,
a hammock from a branch.

The cry of a child;

abandoning the planting
she gave her breast to the child;

the betel-filled mouth
glistening red

she returns to the field
again,
the cry of a child.

திரிதல்

எதிர் எதிராக அமர்ந்து கொள்கிறோம்
யன்னல்கள் எல்லாம் சிறகுகளாக
விரைகிறது ரயில்.
சிதறிப்
பறந்தன வண்ணத்துப் பூச்சிகள்
விட்டு விட்டுத்
தொடர்கிறது வயல்வெளி.

இன்னும்,
கடலும் அழகு, மலையும் அழகு
நதியும்கூட அழகுதான்
எல்லாம்
எங்கள் இருப்பில்
அர்த்தம் கொள்ளும்.

Roaming

We sit across from each other.
The windows become wings,
as the train races;
disturbed,
the butterflies flutter;
fields pass by,
reappear.

Still,
the sea is lovely, the mountains are lovely;
the river too is lovely.
All,
in our posture,
gather meaning.

Exile

மூத்தோன்

மரங்களற்ற பனிக் காட்டில்
தனித்தேன்

நகரத்தின் பெரும் அங்காடிகளில்
வாங்கிப் புனைந்த தடித்த காலணிக்குள்
பாதம் வெடிக்கிறது

குருதிக் காட்சியில் நிலை குலையும்
என் சித்தம் என்பதில்
பெருகும் அச்சத்துடன்
மிகுந்த தயக்கத்துடன்
என் காலடிகளைத் திரும்பிப் பார்க்கிறேன்

அவையோ
மறுமொழி தெரியாத கேள்விகளைத்
தொடர்ந்தும் வீசிய வண்ணம் உள்ளன

முன்னே
பனிப்பாறைகள் அடர்ந்து
நீர் கண்ணாடி இழைகளாய்த் தூங்கும்
    என்னை ஊடுருவு
    துருவிச் செல்
    வெளிபடா இரகசியம் வெளிக்கும்
என்று உறுமுகிறது

மரங்களற்ற வெள்ளைப் பனிக் காட்டில்
தனித்தேன்

உயிர் பிழிந்து உருகிக் குரல் எழுப்பினாலும்
கேட்பவர் இல்லை

The Elder

I stand alone
in a desolate expanse of snow.

My soles sore and bleeding,
wearing thick shoes
the city in its huge factories
makes and churns out.

Knowing how unsettling
the sight of blood can be,
fearfully,
reluctantly,
I inspect my soles.

They reveal nothing,
flinging back
unanswerable questions.

Ahead
mountains of snow,
hanging streamers of glass
speak to me:
"Pierce me
and pass through
hidden truths will emerge."

I stand alone
in a desolate expanse of snow.

No one to hear
the cry of desolation;

‘பயந்த தனிவழிக்குத் துணையென’
எவ்வெழுத்தும் இல்லை.

திடீரென்று
என் எதிரே வருகிறான்
நரை படர்ந்த நீண்ட கூந்தலில்
பனிப் பூக்கள் சொரிந்திருக்க
கழுகின் இறகுகள் சூடி

முகத்திலும் மார்பிலும் வண்ணங்கள் தீட்டி
கையில் நெருப்புச் சட்டியுடன் வருகிறான்
அவன்: மூத்தோன்.

சிறு புகை மூட்டி
இறகுகளை அதில் தோய்த்து
என் பாதங்களை வருடுகிறான்
வலியும் குருதியும் விறைப்பும்
தொலைந்து போகின்றன

என் காலணிகளைத் தூர வீசி எறிகிறேன்

> சினம் மிக்க உன்பாடல்களை எறி
> அவை நெருப்பு மூட்டும்
> அந்த நெருப்பில் நடந்து
> இந்த வெளியை மீறு

என்று திரும்பி நடக்கிறான்

பனிக் காற்றில் அவனுடைய நீண்ட கூந்தல்
அலைகிறது
புன்னகையுடன் என் காலடியைத்
திரும்பிப் பார்க்கிறேன்.

no words to offer
comfort on a solitary path.

Suddenly he appears
across my path;
gray long hair
Speckled with snow
eagle feathers around his neck.

Colours drawn across
his face and chest,
a bowl of fire in his hands,
he comes: the Elder.

He makes a small fire;
with feathers
warmed by the flames,
he strokes my soles;
the pain, the blood and the numbness
disappear.

I fling my shoes away.

"Scatter your angry songs,
they will ignite;
walk on the fire
and cross this plain."

He walks away.

His hair waves
in the cold air;
smiling,
I look at my soles.

காதல் வரி

இலைகள் உதிர்த்து உதிர்த்து
மாரி நெடுந்துயிலிற்குத் தயாராகும்
குளிர்கால மரங்களின் மேல்
மூச்செறிகிறது
இன்னும் தலை நிமிராத நிலவு.

ஹேக் நகரின்
இச் 'சமாந்தர வீதி' யில்
273ஆம் இலக்க வீட்டின்
முன்னறை
சிறிது புதிது
சுவரில் வான் கோவின் பூமரம்.

இரவு விளக்கின் மெல்லிய ஒளி
கசிந்து
கதிரையின் முதுகின்மீது
விசிறப்பட்டுக் கிடக்கும்
மார்ப்புக் கச்சையின்மீது படர்கிறது.

காது மடல்களின் பின்புறம்
இதழ்கள் தொட
மனம் இழைந்து
உடல் அவிழ்ந்து
பொறி கிளம்பித்
தீ பிறந்தது.
காட்டுத் தீயெனப் பற்றி எரிந்தோம்.
தணல் பறந்து
தகித்த வெப்பத்தில்
வெளியே உறைபனியும் உருகிற்று.

Love Song

Leaves fall and fall
as winter's slumber approaches;
on cold-smitten trees
breathes
the nascent moon.

In the Hague
along this Parallel Weg
house number 273
the front room;
somewhat newer
Van Gogh's Flowers
on the wall.

The night lamp's gentle light
seeps and falls
on the brassiere
draped
across the back of the chair.

Lips touch
behind ears,
the heart melts
the body unwraps
sparks ignite
a fire.
We exploded into a forest fire;
the snow outside
melts in the
heat of our passion.

மொழியைக்
கண்களும் உடலும் எடுத்துக்கொண்ட
பிற்பாடு
சொற்கள் உறைந்தன.
பின்
உருகி அனுங்கலாயின
இடையிட்ட மௌனத்தின் அர்த்தப்
பிரவாகமோ
்முடிவிலி வரை,

நீராய்ப் பெருகி
நதியாய் நகர்ந்து
கடலாய்ப் பரந்து செறிந்தோம்.

செயலிழந்து, உடைந்துபோன
காலைக் கடிகாரத்தின் நுண்ணிய
பகுதிகள்,
இலையுதிர் காலத்தில்
உதிர்ந்து சிதறிய சருகுகள்
இவற்றோடு வீசியெறியப்பட்டுக் கிடந்தன
புலன்கள்.

காமனின் கண்ணி வெடி
உயிர் பிளந்து உதிக்கிறது
காதல்
புதிதாக

ஒருபோது நான் நானில்லை
பெண்ணானேன்.
நீ என்னுள் நுழையப்
புலன் மயங்கிற்று
புவியீர்ப்பை எதிர்த்து
ஒரு முடிவற்ற நீர்வீழ்ச்சிதான்

Language
consumed by eyes and body;
later
words froze
then
melted and whimpered;
the silence in between
expands
forever.

A rising flood
a moving river
expands into a sea.

A broken, lifeless
alarm clock
its minute parts
little twigs scattered
in the fall,
with these lie amok
the senses.

Cupid's mines
exploding life,
love
begins again.

One moment of dissolution
I became a woman.
As you entered me
my senses swooned,
defying gravity;
an endless waterfall
I recognize myself,
become a man.

நானென உணர்ந்தேன்
மறுபோது ஆணானேன்
இரவின் சங்கீதம்
நடம் புரிகிற
இரு உடல்
வெளி
எரிகிற நிலவு
இன்னும் உதிரும் சருகு.

பெருங்காற்றில் உழன்ற
மூங்கில் காடு போலக்
குழம்பிற்று கூந்தல்
விரகம் எரித்த இரவு

விடியலாய் வெளிற
காதல் தீ தணிந்து
உடல் அவிய
கண்ணிருண்டு துவண்டேன்
எனினும்
துயில் இன்றல்ல
நாளை

அதுவரை சுழலும் உலகம் தான் அச்சில் மாறிச்
சுழல்க சுழல்க
ஒளிரும் கண்ணும் உடலும் இன்னும்
மலர்க மலர்க.

the night's music,
two lives
in a dance
outside;
a bright moon
twigs still fall.

A bamboo forest
caught in a gale,
the hair asunder
lust burning night.

As it dawns
the fire subsides,
the body hot,
drowsy and restless
yet,
sleep not today
but tomorrow.

Until then
the globe on its axis
continues to turn;
the brightening eyes and body
continue to flower.

மழைக் காட்டின் பெருமரம்

கடலும் மலையும் மழைக்காடுகளும் சேர்ந்திருக்கும்
ஒரு அற்புத உலகத்தில்
மிக மென்மையான குளிரில்
தரையில் நிற்கிறேன்
என் காலடி ஈரம்

பெருக்கின் போது கடல் வந்து போன உயிர்ச்சுவடுகள்
மணல் கோலங்களாகக் கிடக்கின்றன
இப்போதும் புதிதாக

மெல்ல மெல்லக் கடலை மூடிக் கொண்டு வருகிறது
ஒரு பெரும் புகார்
கடல் எது வானம் எது நிலம் எது
என்று தெரியாத
ஒரு மந்திரப் பொழுது பிறக்கிறது

அப்பொழுது வழி தெரியாமல் தத்தளிக்கப் போகும்
தோணிகளுக்குக் குரல் காட்டத்
துறைமுகச் சங்கு விட்டு விட்டு முழங்குகிறது

பெரும்புகார் இப்போது மலைகளையும்
மழைக் காடுகளையும் மூடுகிறது

கொலம்பஸின் கோடரிக்கும் தப்பி
ஆயிரம் வருடங்களாக ஓங்கி நிற்கும்
இந்த நானூறு அடி உயரச் சீடார் மரத்தைப்
புகர் மூட முயல்கிற போது

யுத்தம் எழுமோ என்று தோன்றியது
ஆனால்
அனுபவம் புடமிட்ட நிறைவின் புன்சிரிப்புடன்
பெருமரம் புகாரைத் தழுவிக் கொள்கிறது
நான் கீழே நிற்கிறேன்.

The Giant Tree in the Rain Forest

A wondrous landscape
where mountain, rain forest and ocean
merge,
the weather mild,
I stand on
the moist earth.

The imprints of
a swelling ocean draw
patterns on the sand;
even now

a heavy fog
smothers the ocean slowly
where the sea ends and land begins
blurred in this magical moment;
the lighthouse siren blares
intermittently
to guide the confused canoes.

The fog now swallows
the mountains and the forests.

Towering four hundred feet,
having survived the axe of Columbus
having lived a thousand years,
the cedar, now threatened by a fog;
does this presage a battle?

Marked by the wisdom of time
the giant tree smiles,
embraces the fog.
I stand below.

காடுகளின் உயிரைத் தன் வேரிலும்
காற்றின் ஆத்மாவைத் தன் முடியிலும்
சுமந்து நிற்கிறது இப் பெருமரம்
வார்த்தைகள் இல்லாவிட்டாலும்
அதன் மூச்சில் இருக்கிறது
வரலாறுகளின் பேச்சு.

பொறுமையில் மலைகளையும் பூமியையும்
புறங்கண்ட பிற்பாடு
வெறி கொண்ட காற்றைச் சாடுவதற்கு
ஒரு சிறு கிளையை மட்டுமே வீசி எறிகிறது.
பெருமரம்

அதன் கீழ்
வெட்டரிவாளுடன் மானுடத்தின்
சிறுமை.

The life of the forest in its roots
the soul of the air in its crown,
the tree,

no tongue to speak,
but in its breath
the tale of history.

Its patience
having vanquished the earth
having spurned the hills,
the giant tree
now flings a branch
to appease the enraged wind.

And below
with chain saws
petty humans stand.

ஒன்பது நாட்கள்

மொழி தெரியாத புதிய பட்டினத்துக்குப்
பறந்தேன்
அங்கு இருந்தது ஒரு நீலக் காற்று
அதன் மொழியின் இனிமையில்
குழைத்த பத்துப் பாடல்கள் எறிந்தேன்

கண்கள் இமைக்கவில்லை
நிலத்தைக் கால் தொடவில்லை
நடந்தேன் பறந்தேன்

பட்டினத்தின் மனிதர்களுக்கு
என் முகம் தெரியவில்லை
காற்றுக்கும் என் பாடல் பிடிபடவில்லை
எனினும்
கோபமும் மென்மையும்
பிணைப்பில் இணைய
ஊடல் சுழன்று எழும் வீச்சில்
என்னைத் தழுவிக் கொண்டது அது

முதல் மூன்று நாட்களும் பகலில்
அடுத்த மூன்று நாட்களும் இரவில்
இறுதி மூன்று நாட்களும் கண்ணீரில் என
விதிக்கப் பட்டிருந்தது காதலுக்கு

நித்திய ஈரலிப்பிலும்
சலிக்காத முத்தத்துடன்
கால்களற்று
எப்போதும் பறக்கும் பறவை நான்

அவளோ
பட்டினத்தின் நவீன இடிபாடுகளிடையும்

Nine Days

I flew
to a new land with a foreign tongue;
a blue wind swept across;
relishing that language
I scattered ten songs.

Unblinking eyes,
feet that do not touch the ground,
I walked and flew.

The people of this land,
failed to see my face;
the wind was bemused
by my song;
yet,
angry and gentle,
in the grip
of a swirling passion
it embraced me.

The first three days in the light
the next three days in the dark,
the last three days in tears,
destiny shaped my love.

Forever moist,
no ebb in my kisses,
without feet,
I am in constant flight.

She,
in the city's constant jolts,

காலக் கிழவனின் முட்களிடையும்
சிக்குண்ட காற்றின்
கூந்தல்.

in the thorns of time,
the tresses
of an entangled wind.

கண்ணாடி மழை

திருப்பங்களற்று நெடுந்தூரம் நீளும்
தெருவின் இரு முனைகளையும்
பேய் அறைந்த அச்சம்
இறுக மூடியிருக்கிறது

எதுவும் நுழையா இரும்புப் போர்வை
அதற்கு மேலே

தெளிவான மொழியில்
சிறப்பு ஆணைகள் தரப்படுகின்றன

பிற்பாடு
எழுத்துப் பிழையற்ற பெயர்ப் பட்டியல்களைக்
கைகளில் தாங்கி
சீரான நடை சீரான உடையில்
ஒரு சீரான அழிவு
அகலக் காலடி எடுத்து வைக்கிறது

தெருவின் இரண்டு பக்கமும்
யன்னல்களும் கதவுகளும் உடைந்து வீழ்கின்றன
கனவு தடம்புரள
விழித்து அலறியவர்கள் மீது
சுவர் இடிந்து சரிகின்றது
நொருங்கிய கண்ணாடி மழை எழுப்பும் ஓலம்
காதுகேளாத பெரும் சங்கீதக்காரனின்
இசைக் கோர்வைகளைக்
குலைத்துப் போடுகையில்

திருப்பங்களற்ற தெரு
நீண்டு, நீண்டு
இப்போது ரயில் பாதையாகின்றது:
முகாம்களுக்குச் செல்லும் ஒருவழிப்பாதை

Glass Rain

A long straight street
at both ends
shut firmly
a deathly fear.

Sealed shut,
above

in precise words
clear instructions.

Later
flawless lists in hand
measured steps,
firmly pressed clothes
measured destruction
takes giant steps.

On both sides of the street
doors and windows crumble
dreams shaken
they wake and scream
as walls topple;
the din of glass rain
destroys the music
of the deaf artist.

The long straight street
now lengthens
becomes a track
a one-way passage
towards the camp

அதில்
நேரகாலமற்று விசித்திரமான அவல ஒலியுடன்
விரைகின்றன ரயில்கள்

இருளும் பகலும் வெளியும் நிலவும்
காடும் கடந்து போவதை அறியாமல்
மூடப்பட்ட பெட்டிகளுள்
நெரிபடுகின்ற மனிதர்களின் கண்கள்
மெல்ல மெல்ல ஒளியிழக்கின்றன

முதலில் சென்ற ரயிலில்
அடைபட்டிருந்தவர்களுக்கு
என்ன நடந்தது என்று தெரியாது
ஆனால்
முகாமுக்குச் சென்ற கடைசி ரயிலில்
குழந்தைகள் மட்டுமே இருந்தனர்
அவர்களிடமும் குரல் எஞ்சவில்லை

எஞ்சியவை

நெருப்புக்காளவாய்க்குத் தப்பிய கொஞ்சம் பொம்மைகள்
கொத்துக் கொத்தாய் தலைமுடி
வாயிலோன் களவாட மறந்த தங்கப் பல்
எரிய மறுத்த ஒரு புகைப்படம்
நொருங்கிய கண்ணாடித்துண்டுகளின் கீழ்
இரவில்
காற்றில் அலையாத சாம்பல்
இறந்தாலும்
மூடமறுத்த இரண்டு கண்கள்.

to which
the trains
screeching incessantly
rush.

In those closed boxes
no longer visible
night and day
land, moon and the woods,
the eyes of the cramped crowd
now glaze over.

Those carried in the first train
knew nothing
but
in the last train to the camp
only children remained
they too had no voice.

What remained:

a few dolls that escaped the furnace
locks of hair
a golden tooth
the guard forgot to steal,
a picture that refused to burn
under the crushed glass
in the night
still ashes
even in death
two eyes refusing to close.

Aftermath

குரல்

நண்ப
ஏன் என்னைக் கேட்டாய்?

துறந்தோர், துறப்போர்
இறந்தோர், இறப்போர்
இருந்தோர், அழிந்தோர்
எழுந்தோர், விழுந்தோர்
நினைத்தோர், மறந்தோர்
மரித்தோர், உயிர்த்தோர்
மிதந்தோர், அலைந்தோர்

இவர்களுள் எத்தனை பேரை
எனக்குத் தெரியும் என
எப்படித் தெரிந்தது உனக்கு?

கடலுக்கு அப்பால் நான் இருந்தாலும்
கணினித் திரையில் குருதி மழை

என்னைச் சூழ உருகி ஓடும் நதியில்
மிதக்கிறது ஒரு பெரும் பனிப்பாறை
அதன்மேல் நனைந்த சிறகுகளுடன்
கிடக்கிறது காயம் பட்ட கடல் காகம்

திசை அறியும் கணிதம் தெரியாதவர்களிடம்
சிக்குண்டது
நதியா, பறவையா?

ஏன் என்னைக் கேட்டாய்?

இருப்பு அழிந்தாலும்
உயிர் எரியும் உன் குரலின்
எதிரொலியைத் திருப்பித் தருவேன் என்றா?

VOICE

Friend:

Why ask me?

Those who lost and will lose
perished and will die
lived and were destroyed
rose and fell
remembered and forgot
succumbed and were born
floated and wandered—

how did you know
how many of them
I knew?

I live beyond the seas
river of blood on my screen.

An iceberg floats
on the melting river around me.
On it
a wounded cormorant
feathers wet.

Trapped
among those who cannot
navigate,
the river or the bird?

Why ask me?

Did you think
the voice of your burning life
having lost all
echoes in mine?

கொலைக்காட்சி

பொய்மையும் வன்மம் சூழ் மாயக் காட்சிகளும்
அவர்களுடைய படையெடுப்பில்
புகையுடன் சேர்ந்து மேலெழுந்தபோது

சொல் பிறழ்ந்தது
படிமங்கள் உடைந்தன
வாழ்க்கை குருதி இழந்தது

எறிகணை பட்டுத் தெறிக்கக்
காயம் பட்ட
இரண்டரை வயதுக் குழந்தையின் கைகளை
மயக்க மருந்தின்றி அறுக்கின்ற மருத்துவன்
இக்கணம் கடவுள்
நீரற்ற விழிகளுடன் அலறும் தாய்
ஒரு பிசாசு.

Massacre

In their onslaught
the lies
the malicious sleight of hand
now joins the smoke

words dissemble
structures crumble
life's blood oozes out.

The shell explodes
a child wounded,
barely two and a half years old;
the doctor
now a god
without an anesthetic
amputates the hands.
The mother screams
tearless eyes
now a demon.

அஞ்சலி

புதையுண்டவர்கள்
எரியுண்டவர்கள்
கடலொடு போனவர்கள்
    எல்லோரதும் தெளிவான, திருத்தமான தகவல்கள்
    உலகப் பணிமனையின்
    நிலத்தடி ஆவணக் காப்பகங்களுக்குப் போய் விட்டன

எங்கள் எல்லோருடைய ஒற்றைப் புதைகுழி மீது
படைத்தளபதியின் கோவணத்தை
தேசியக் கொடியாக ஏற்றுகிறார்கள்

எங்கள் கண்ணீர் எழுப்பிய நினைவுச் சின்னத்தில்
ஒருவர் வெற்று வார்த்தைகளை எழுதுகிறார்

பலர் கனவுகளைப் பின்னுகிறார்கள்

மௌனம் கலையாமல்
அவன் கவிதையை எழுதுகிறான்.

Tribute

Buried
burned
flung into the sea
their clear and precise data
now safely stored
in the world's archives.

On our mass grave
the General's loin-cloth
flies like a national flag.

On the altar of our tears
words that signify nothing.

So many dreamers.

Unperturbed
he writes his poem.

உடல்

கடலோரம் தலை பிளந்து கிடந்த
உடல்.

இறப்பிலும் மூட மறுத்த கண்களின்
நேர் கொண்ட பார்வையில் மிதக்கிறது:
எதிர்ப்பு, ஆச்சரியம், தவிப்பு,
தத்தளிப்பு, கொதிப்பு, ஆற்றாமை,
முடிவற்ற ஒரு பெருங்கனவு.

The Body

Along the shore
a body,
a smashed head;
eyes resolutely open
even in death,
in the gaze:
defiance, surprise, grief, turmoil, anger, despair.
An endless dream.

தலைமுறை

ஒரு தலைமுறைக்கு முன்
நாடு கடந்தார்கள்
அடுத்த தலைமுறை மெல்ல மெல்ல மொழி இழக்கும்
தருணத்தில்
தீராப்பெருவலி எழுந்து எம்மை இணைக்கிறது

பனி உதிர்ந்து காற்றுறையும் இரவுப் பெரும் பொழுதிலும்
சினத்துடன் எழுந்து தெருவை நிறைத்த
பல்லாயிரம் மக்களிடையே
குரல் வற்றிய ஒரு பெண்ணைக் கண்டேன்

கண்ணீரின் சுவடுகளால் முகக் கோலம் அழிந்தாலும்
இன்னொரு முகம் பன்முகமாக விரியக் கண்டேன்.

Generations

A generation ago
they left their land;
as the next generation
begins to lose
its language
an unbearable pain
now brings us together.

Where snow falls
and the air freezes
even in the night
among those
rising in anger
blocking the streets
I see a girl
her voice gone hoarse.

The marks of tears
disfigure her face;
another face multiplies
and blossoms.

காணி நிலம்

இந்தக் காணி நிலத்தில் என்னுடைய கதை பிறந்தது

அங்கு கடல் கொண்ட பெருமரங்களின்
வேரடிமண் இப்பொது வெளித் தெரிகிறது

கோடை காலத்திலும் ஈர மனிதர்
உலவித் திரிந்த நிலம்
ஒரு சில நாட்களில்
மொழி பெயர் தேயமாக மாறுகிறது

இந்தக் காணி நிலத்தில் தென்னைகள் இல்லை
குடிசைகள் இல்லை
கிளைக் கதைகள் சிறைப்பட்டுப் போனபிற்பாடும்

முடிவற்ற கதை இது என்று சொல்கிறது
குரல்.

A Plot of Land

On this plot of land
my story began.

There the sea-swept
giant trees stand
the subsoil
now exposed.

It was a land in which
under a blazing sun
kind people walked;
in a few days
its language is lost.

On this plot of land
no coconut trees
no huts.
Even the stories
are now captive;
yet

a voice insists:
this is
a tale
that does not end.

காடாற்று

வெந்து தணியாத
காடாற்றச் சென்றோம்
ஒரு குருவி கிடையாது

ஆள்காட்டி வெளிக்குமேல்
ஆகாயம் இல்லை

கண் தொட முடியாத எல்லைவரை
சாம்பல் வீசிக் கிடக்கின்ற நிலமற்ற நிலத்தில்
எலும்புகளைத் தேட
ஒருவருக்கும் வழி இல்லை

எனினும்

பாலூற்ற ஊற்றப் பெருகும்
எம் கண்ணீரைக் கேளிக்கையாக்கி
கொண்டாட்டத்தோடு
களிக்கூத்து ஆடும்
மாற்றான் குலத்துக்கு
நம்
மாற்றுவழி என்ன?

இதயப் பெருந்தீயைக் குளிர்விக்க
இன்றைக்கு ஒன்றுமில்லை

காயாத குருதித்துளிக்கு
சாட்சியம் இல்லை

முற்றிற்று என்று சொல்லி
காற்றிலும் கடலிலும் கரைத்துவிட்டுக்

Healing the Forest

To heal a still
smoldering land,
we went;
no bird in sight.

An empty sky
above the sparrow-flying
earth.

An ash-covered landless earth
to the edge of that wide expanse;
here, no one knows
how to gather bones.

Yet,

Our libation of milk
the relentless
welling of tears
now mocked with glee
with dance and song
by an estranged foe;
what then is the
way ahead?

To cool the burning heart
there is nothing today.

No witness
for the drop of blood
still not dry.

To claim closure
to dissolve ashes in the sea
to scatter in the air
to close one's eyes,

கண்மூட
காற்றும் கிடையாது
கடலும் கிடையாது
காடாற்று எப்போதோ?

there is no air
there is no sea
there is no way
to heal the forest.